W9-DJF-236

NEW DIRECTIONS FOR ADULT AND CONTINUING EDUCATION

Susan Imel, *Ohio State University*
EDITOR-IN-CHIEF

Understanding and Negotiating the Political Landscape of Adult Education

Catherine A. Hansman
Cleveland State University

Peggy A. Sissel
University of Arkansas at Little Rock

EDITORS

Number 91, Fall 2001

JOSSEY-BASS
A Wiley Company
www.josseybass.com

UNDERSTANDING AND NEGOTIATING THE POLITICAL LANDSCAPE OF ADULT
EDUCATION
Catherine A. Hansman, Peggy A. Sissel (eds.)
New Directions for Adult and Continuing Education, no. 91
Susan Imel, Editor-in-Chief

Microfilm copies of issues and articles are available in 16mm and 35mm,
as well as microfiche in 105mm, through University Microfilms Inc., 300
North Zeeb Road, Ann Arbor, Michigan 48106-1346.

ISSN 1052-2891   ISBN 07879-5775-5

NEW DIRECTIONS FOR ADULT AND CONTINUING EDUCATION is part of The
Jossey-Bass Higher and Adult Education Series and is published quarterly
by Jossey-Bass, 989 Market Street, San Francisco, California 94103.

SUBSCRIPTIONS cost $59.00 for individuals and $114.00 for institutions,
agencies, and libraries.

EDITORIAL CORRESPONDENCE should be sent to the Editor-in-Chief,
Susan Imel, ERIC/ACVE, 1900 Kenny Road, Columbus, Ohio
43210-1090. E-mail: imel.1@osu.edu.

Cover photograph by Wernher Krutein/PHOTOVAULT <\#169> 1990.

www.josseybass.com

Printed in the United States of America on acid-free recycled paper con-
taining 100 percent recovered waste paper, of which at least 20 percent
is postconsumer waste.

CONTENTS

EDITORS' NOTES

The political landscape of adult education is rough terrain, made more so by the decisions and issues in adult education practice that are inherently political. These political decisions encompass embedded issues and power struggles with which adult educators grapple but do not necessarily give voice to in their everyday practice. In this volume, we seek to make more visible what is known but not discussed: the politics of the work of adult education.

Our actions as adult educators require us to interact among competing interests and power in our day-to-day practice. As coeditors, we believe that no form of education is neutral and that as educators we must develop a critical perspective about the potentially conflictual and political nature of our work. An exciting theoretical base analyzing the political nature of education is already in place. Our purpose for this volume is to draw from this theoretical base, give voice to the multiple ways of approaching political issues in the field of adult education, and contribute to the understanding of both macro- and micropolitical environments that are part of our everyday work. Thus, this volume focuses on the politics of adult education from a variety of perspectives.

Our intent is to provide readers with a diversity of insights into the politics and policy issues that surround them in the field. Grounded in both theory and practice, each of the chapters identifies and critiques a specific area of the politics of adult education and suggests strategies for reflection and action while working in this highly political world. Chapters examine the political aspects of higher education, adult educators in K–12-focused colleges of education, literacy education, social welfare reform, professional organizations, and identity of the field.

In Chapter One, Peggy Sissel lays the foundation for the political analysis in this volume. She examines and analyzes what is political in adult education, drawing on the literature of the politics of education to build a political framework to analyze adult education policies, programs, and practices.

Chapters Two through Four examine the political struggles that adult educators frequently encounter while practicing within higher education. In Chapter Two, Sissel, Catherine Hansman, and Carol Kasworm detail the limited power, privilege, and advocacy that adult learners encounter in higher education. They challenge all adult educators to take action to question hegemonic policies that confront adult learners on higher education campuses. Chapter Three, authored by Scipio Colin and Tom Heaney, furthers this discussion by arguing that democratic practice in adult education concerns both content and process. The challenge to create participatory practice within higher education and adult education graduate programs inevitably involves anticipating and countering resistance and pushing borders. Using examples from their graduate adult education classes and programs, they show that democracies are not totalizing structures, that they always exist in the midst of contradictory and hegemonic institutions, and that it is through engagement with these structures that genuine participation and democracy are obtained. In Chapter Four, Michael Day, Donna Amstutz, and Donna Whitson address the tension and political realities inherent in graduate adult education programs housed in university colleges of education. This tension stems from five sources: beliefs about knowledge, schools, learning, teaching, and issues surrounding resource allocation. Through the presentation of issues and dilemmas they faced in their own graduate program, they discuss possible compromises within colleges of education that may result in increased voice for graduate adult education programs.

Chapters Five and Six address the politics of literacy education. Barbara Sparks's feminist analysis in Chapter Five unpacks how gender is constructed and maintained through the Adult Education and Family Literacy Act; she argues that family has been pulled into the public domain for regulating the educational development of children. Thus, women's literacy development and personal goals have been sacrificed and subordinated to the needs of the family and a patriarchal system. Sparks contends that future research and feminist policy analysis should focus on exposing power differences and inequality that result in competing interests between women's development for parenting and women's development for work. B. Allan Quigley in Chapter Six likens the lives of literacy educators to feudal farmers in describing the confusing and hegemonic polices that confront both learners and educators in literacy. He points to new trends in political negotiations of literacy education that may lead to the democratization of knowledge in literacy education.

The final three chapters address political issues in professional organizations and identity of the field. In Chapter Seven, Phyllis Cunningham explores the politics and policies (or lack thereof) of the American Association for Adult and Continuing Education. She analyzes the participatory nature of the organization, the dominant ideology as expressed by the leadership and in its conference programming, and how knowledge about issues is or is not cultivated, suggesting that leadership is needed to span the ideological space of the different factions of adult education so adult educators can work together. In Chapter Eight, Arthur Wilson discusses the issues of identity and power that confront adult educators on all fronts. Adult education as a field has used applied rigorous scientific research to help achieve identity. Wilson maintains that the central political problem to constituting professional identity is one of controlling access to professions and the training of professionals—something that adult education has not achieved to date. He suggests three strategies to help build identity as adult educators: forging occupational alliances with other professions, becoming reflective practitioners by adding a reflective dimension to training for adult educators, and becoming more politically engaged. In the concluding chapter, Catherine Hansman highlights and discusses the political issues raised by the previous chapter authors. She asserts that adult education as a field can influence the larger world only if we adult educators recognize the political nature of all their work, negotiating and compromising on conflicts while respecting the philosophical and ideological pluralism that is well established in the field.

In the limited space of this volume, we recognize that many aspects of the political landscape of adult education have been left out. Nevertheless, we believe that the issues raised by the chapter authors can add to awareness and discussions concerning the political landscape of adult education while encouraging important new lines of research and analysis. To become more politically engaged, adult educators from all areas must recognize the political dimensions of their practices. We hope that the chapters in this volume will aid adult educators in reflecting on and sharing the political challenges they confront in their everyday practice of adult education.

Catherine A. Hansman
Peggy A. Sissel
Editors

CATHERINE A. HANSMAN *is associate professor and program director of the M.Ed. program in adult learning and development and the leadership and lifelong learning track in the Ph.D. program in urban education at Cleveland State University, Ohio.*

PEGGY A. SISSEL *is a researcher and consultant with the Center for Applied Studies in Education at the University of Arkansas at Little Rock.*

1

An analysis of the political aspects of adult education reveals multiple ways of examining the policies, programs, and practices that shape the roles of adult educators. This chapter presents a framework designed to encourage critical reflection about how the political landscape affects adult educators' work and lives, as well as ways that adult educators can affect change in that terrain.

Thinking Politically: A Framework for Adult and Continuing Education

Peggy A. Sissel

"It's all political!" This common phrase, simple in its syntax and succinct in its assertion, has the capacity to sum up the conflicts, constraints, conundrums, and inequities that ultimately shape social relations among people, within organizations, and, more broadly, between collectives of interested parties. These collectives can be as large and diverse as a nation-state, as small as a family unit, or as specific as an individual program (Sissel, 2000) or field of study (Marshall and Scribner, 1991). Indeed, politics and concepts of the political are not restricted to activities of governments or partisan electoral politics. Rather, politics functions within both private and public spheres and in all settings influenced by power—in other words, all aspects of the human condition (West and Blumberg, 1990).

Perhaps it is because political analysis can be applied in any human context that the broad utterance, "It's all political," became so firmly established in our vernacular. In addition, the multiple levels of analysis it connotes fit intuitively into our experience of living in a world contested by racism, sexism, classism, and other ways of demarcating and deprecating others. For instance, as an expression of cynicism, this colloquialism critiques and summarizes perceived uses and misuses of power. As a metaphor, it alludes to central issues embedded within the political frame, including the acquisition, allocation, and distribution of resources and the constraints and struggles over competing ideologies and differing perspectives. Finally, as an informal assessment, it provides a shared meaning about the outcome of a given set of social relations, particularly as it relates to issues of inequity, notions of fairness, and concepts of justice.

NEW DIRECTIONS FOR ADULT AND CONTINUING EDUCATION, no. 91, Fall 2001   © John Wiley & Sons, Inc.

If the premise is that "it's all political," then the question of what is political about adult and continuing education looms large. The chapter authors in this volume have approached this question in differing ways, yet the themes of identity and ideology, privilege and power, accommodation and resistance, and resources and strategy lie at the core of their commentary. This chapter explores the basic premises of a political analysis and why this framework is useful for adult education. In it, I argue that by thinking politically about adult education practice, programs, and policies, expanded possibilities for critically reflective practice, communal discourse, and strategic planning emerge, as do possibilities for active engagement in advocacy for adult learners, ourselves, and our field.

Aspects of the Political

According to Ginsburg (2000), politics and education can be conceptualized in two distinct but interconnected ways: "the politics of education and the political work accomplished through education" (p. ix). A brief look at adult education history reveals the vast array of accomplishment and literature regarding the latter type. Political work through the education of adults can readily be found, historically and contemporaneously, in areas such as immigration, literacy, civil rights, gay rights, racism, gender equality, the environment, international development, health, and criminal justice (Freire, 1970; Adams, 1975; Hall, 1978; Addams, 1996; Beder, 1996; Sissel and Hohn, 1996; Wangoola and Youngman, 1996; Coben, 1998; Ewert and Grace, 2000; Baird, 2001; Grace, 2001). Examples of organizations at the forefront of this work are the Highlander Folk School, the Doris Marshall Institute, World Education, and the International Council on Adult Education.

This rich history of political work through adult education not only reveals its potential but begs the broader question that Ginsburg alludes to: What constitutes the politics of adult education? Several scholars have sought to address this question from a macropolitical perspective. In particular, Jarvis's (1993) theoretical framework of the politics of adult education in relation to the nation-state, Wangoola and Youngman's (1996) collection of essays on the political economy of adult education, and most recently, Jeria's (2001) analysis of the global economy and its influence on adult learning have contributed to the critical discourse regarding geopolitical aspects of the field.

Programmatically, Cervero and Wilson's analysis of the politics of program planning (1994) and Quigley's work (1994), which links the politics of literacy policy to practice, are examples of scholarship that bridge the theoretical and pragmatic aspects of the politics of adult education. Deshler and Grudens-Schuck's (2000) inquiry into the politics of epistemology traces the theoretical underpinnings of knowledge production while moving the discourse to the dailiness of practitioners' lives. My research on the influence of macropolitics on the micropolitics within both informal and formal educational settings and its effect on outcomes further extends the political analysis of adult education (Sissel, Birdsong, and Silaski, 1997; Sissel, 2000).

One aspect of the politics of adult education addressed frequently in the literature has been the notion of power and privilege and its corollary construct: powerlessness and marginality. The past decade has seen the emergence of this focus on power relationships in adult education settings, particularly in relation to gender, class, and race biases (Hart, 1992; Tisdell, 1993; Flannery, 1994; Sheared, 1994; Cunningham, 1996; Johnson-Bailey and Cervero, 1996, 2000; Sissel, Birdsong, and Silaski, 1997; Rocco and West, 1998; Sissel, 2000; Sheared and Sissel, 2001).

These scholars and others point to the necessity of developing an analysis of adult education that encompasses not only social and cultural dimensions but microsocial theories of learning and teaching as well. Scholars in the broader field of the politics of education, such as Ball (1987) and Blase (1991a), have pointed out that macrolevel social, political, and cultural factors all influence the micropolitics of educational settings. Thus, the micropolitics of educational organizations and the teaching and learning that take place within them cannot be understood without some comprehension of the external environment in which they function.

Furthermore, politics of education has other dimensions in addition to power. While Blase (1991b) has remarked that "central to all perspectives on micro-politics is the use of power" (p. 185), Hoyle (1986), Blase (1991a), Iannaconne (1975, 1991), Ball (1987), Bolman and Deal (1991), and Ginsburg, Kamat, Raghu, and Weaver (1995) cite other distinct factors that also affect sociopolitical relations in organizations, among them goal diversity, ideological disputes, conflict of interests, political activity, control, visibility, material conditions, and ethics. Thus, politics, which is intimately linked to power, is also concerned with these constructs, each of which contributes to the manifestation of power and control, particularly as it relates to the acquisition of and use of material and symbolic resources with and for learners.

Key Issues Within the Politics of Adult Education

As Hall (1978) has summarized, all serious educational movements are political. Yet I would argue that many educators do not think of their work as political or having political dimensions. Following are five key issues within the politics of adult education that I believe are vital to thinking politically: dimensions of diversity, conflicts of interest, material conditions and control, political activity through accommodation and resistance, and strategic thinking and visibility.

Multiple Dimensions: The Politics of Diversity. To think politically is to think critically about the forces that shape how we think about what we do: the ideologies we embrace or reject and the goals we seek. Adult education as a field of scholarship and practice has never represented a singular or unitary perspective or programming emphasis, as evidenced by the periodic dissolution and restructuring of adult education associations and collectives (see Chapters Seven and Eight, this volume). Twenty years ago, Kreitlow and his associates (1981) examined some of the controversies affecting the field and the distinct ideologies framing perspectives about issues ranging from mandatory continuing education to venues of program planning. Zinn's work (1999) explicating a typology of educational philosophies expressed by adult educators and Merriam's (1995) edited volume that addressed the foundations of these perspectives are also indicative of the ideological divisions within adult education. And most recently, Tisdell and Taylor (2001) have examined the influence of philosophy on practice.

In the 1990s, the infusion of feminist theories, postmodern analyses, and multicultural critiques was, for some, a welcome addition to this discourse of difference. Others, however, viewed these new, discursive elements as lacking value, or as threatening (Sissel and Sheared, 2001). Cunningham's (2001) commentary on the 1992 Adult Education Research Conference in Saskatoon reveals the point at which the forms and forums of this discourse took a different turn. What had been a theoretical dialogue now took on activist dimensions, as the growing numbers of women and people of color in the field asserted their rights to be visible within the literature.

It is not surprising that the political activity Cunningham (2001) describes took place as the faces of the field began to change. As Bolman and Deal (1991) have observed, "Politics and political behavior is more visible and dominant under conditions of diversity than of homogeneity" (p. 188). More so than at any other time, the 1990s saw the meaning of diversity in the field expanded beyond that of programming and ideology, to include not only issues of race, class, and gender but also new pedagogies, epistemologies, and research practices. Because of this ever-increasing diversity, it is imperative that a new discourse about our commonalties be developed and new ways of constructing collectives be forged if we are to develop voices of advocacy for adult learners. This may happen within—or without—what we now perceive as the field. If it does not occur, either among ourselves or through linkages with other collectives, most assuredly others will step into the void to mediate the needs of learners in ways that we may be opposed to.

Whose Interest?   To think politically is to think critically about the expectations we hold about learners, ourselves, and others with whom we work. While the politics of diversity affects our collective way of being, diversity issues also influence our interactions with learners. The assumptions we hold about adult learners need to move beyond models and frameworks based on theories derived from white middle-class learners in the 1960s (Hayes and Colin, 1994). Research into generation X (Sacks, 1996; Wagschal, 1997), as well as research regarding women (Hayes and Flannery, 2000) and differing cultural groups (Harper, 2001), indicates that theories such as andragogy (Knowles, 1970) may be the result of cohort and cultural effects rather than a universal norm.

These emerging insights into adult development and learning are not merely theoretical; they have political implications as well. When adult educators, individually or collectively, choose to honor or ignore new information about differing cultures, learning styles, ways of knowing, or contextual influences, they are acting politically. These choices, whether actions or omissions, function as political acts because they either perpetuate or challenge existing power relations (Ginsburg, Kamat, Raghu, and Weaver, 1995).

In response, critical reflection by adult educators should include a focus on how our individual and collective knowledge base influences the assumptions, biases, and expectations that we hold about learners and how these views are played out in day-to-day practices (Rist, 1970; Giroux, 1981; Tisdell, 1993; Ginsburg, Kamat, Raghu, and Weaver, 1995). Only when adult educators embrace a true commitment to try to understand the lived experiences and perspectives that diverse learners bring to educational settings can the interests of both the educator and the learner be at the center (Sissel, 1997; Bounous, 2001). Without this commitment to the political act of engaging in the multicultural literature and life world of learners, then only the interests of the educator are placed in the center. This expanded perspective of community, as Galbraith (1990) points out, is critical to creating in learners "a sense of hope and dignity, a sense of responsibility for their own communities and lives, and a voice in the social and political arenas" (pp. 7–8).

Material Conditions and Control. To think politically is to think critically about how our role as adult educators is constructed and about the working conditions of our lived experiences as adult educators that are the result of programmatic priorities, expectations and mandates, and organizational and institutional contexts and cultures. Certainly, our expectations and assumptions about learners influence the choices we make about our practice (Tisdell, 1993; Ginsburg, Kamat, Raghu, and Weaver, 1995; Sissel, 1997); nevertheless, as the chapter authors in this volume attest, external influences such as policies, funding, accountability issues, and lack of visibility are at the forefront of concerns among adult educators. Each of these issues influences our perceptions of what may be possible not only for and with learners but as it relates to our own professional growth and development as practitioners and scholars.

Educational practice and programming are carried out within the parameters of policy and in response and in relation to the material conditions, human interests, diversity of goals, perceptions of power, and ethics that those very policies have circumscribed (Ball, 1987). Thus, our social relations with learners and each other are affected by the development of policy and all that ensues as a result of its creation. This includes the development and interpretation of programmatic mission and goals, the appropriation and allocation of funding, the selection of curricula, decisions around implementation of programming, and the assessment of programmatic outcomes.

This linkage between the macropolitical policy and funding climate and the programmatic constraints within the adult basic literacy education and general equivalency diploma organization has been examined by Quigley (1994), Cuban and Hayes, (1996), Amstutz (2001), and others. In this volume, Chapters Five and Six critique aspects of this fundamental function of adult education. Yet although this issue has been well addressed in adult literacy practice, other contexts of adult learning also need to be understood better.

Clearly, the way in which policy gets transformed into practice is highly political and often idiosyncratic, yet the mechanisms at play are not well researched. Foucault (1980) identified two sets of concerns in this realm: the political relations of power (what goes on between people) and the ethical (one's actions in relation to the institution). Our actions as educators and the kinds of daily practice decisions that we make may be the result of one's role in the system; thus, we must affix moral responsibilities to policies and our actions (Cervero and Wilson, 1994). Within the context of human resource development, Garrick and Solomon (2001) and Childs (2001) have recently examined the macropolitical forces that shape daily practice, while tying them to the politics of power and ethics. Other contexts analyzed from this approach include higher education for adults (Kasworm, Sandmann, and Sissel, 2000) and parent involvement in Head Start (Sissel, 1997, 2000). Each of these works illuminates some aspects of the interplay of policy, programming, and practice. Such continued research into the interstitial link between the macropolitical and the micropolitical worlds of adult educators has potential for helping adult educators understand how best to negotiate the political landscape at the national, state, local, and programmatic levels.

Political Activity: Accommodation and Resistance. To think politically is to think critically about how we negotiate, accommodate, or resist hegemonic structures, frameworks, and practices. Kreisberg (1992), in his work on power in educational settings, observed that "resistance is readily apparent in most situations of domination. While the mechanisms of hegemony are powerful, they are not all-encompassing, and they are always characterized by contradictions and conflict" (p. 16).

Thus, essential to understanding politics in adult education is our comprehension of the concepts of accommodation and resistance and the development of a critical perspective that helps us understand the contradictions and conflicts that shape our practices (Brookfield, 2000). The political frame recognizes that as we as educators negotiate our day-to-day reality, we either accommodate and reproduce the structural and ideological frameworks of the institutions in which we work or we engage in action that resists and seeks to transform it (Aronowitz and Giroux, 1993).

Giroux (1983) has pointed to both the reality and dailiness of resistance-in-practice in his critique of analyses of the functions of schooling and pedagogical processes within educational institutions. According to Giroux, acts of resistance are forms of refusal against domination and submission. Furthermore, oppositional behaviors have differing levels of effectiveness and importance, and differing magnitudes of strength for creating liberatory spaces. In fact, as he and others illustrate, some forms of resistance are actually contradictory and lead to accommodation of oppressive structures and social relations (Willis, 1981; Giroux, 1983; Apple, 1995; Sissel, 2000), thereby perpetuating conditions of exploitation. Such analyses of accommodation and resistance center the subject as being part of a broader framework of social realities and identities and situate the self in raced, classed, and gendered positions of power and privilege, powerlessness or oppression.

Considering the marginalized status of adult educators, such analyses of accommodation of or resistance to hegemony are instructive because of the way in which they illuminate the paradox of our perceptions. Immersed in our daily individual and collective practices, we may believe that we are engaging in emancipatory practices, while unwittingly contributing to the creation and perpetuation of structures that are anything but liberatory.

As Giroux (1983) has pointed out, "Human agency and structures come together most visibly at the point where oppositional practices and meanings contribute to the very nature of the hegemonic process. Such resistance reveals not only the active side of hegemony, it also provides the basis for a radical pedagogy that would make it the object of a critical deciphering and analysis" (p. 165).

Strategic Thinking: Politics of Resources. To think politically is to think strategically for purposes of change making, increased visibility, better advocacy around the issues that learners face, programmatic needs and funding initiatives, personal and professional growth and development, and greater voice for the field. This entails the development of a strategy around the "tactical use of power to retain or obtain control of real or symbolic resources" (Blase, 1991, p. 288).

As Chapter Two in this volume notes, it is difficult to acquire resources when the need is not visible, understood, or accepted. Relatedly, Chapter Seven asserts the need for a professional association for the field that produces policy papers around a range of issues pertinent to adult learners. Some issues ripe for analysis and advocacy are societal influences on adult learning participation patterns, such as the loss of leisure, changes in family structure, the graying of the population, shifts in immigration patterns, welfare reform, and economic changes due to the global economy.

Conclusion

Each of the chapter authors offers suggestions for ways of thinking about the politics of adult education and strategies at the practice, program, and policy levels. These include analyses of adult educators and adult learners within higher education (Chapter Two), the role of adult educators within colleges of education (Chapter Four), and the process of democratic participation in graduate programs for adults (Chapter Three). Two different views of the policy dimension of adult literacy education (Chapters Five and Six) are provided, and the professional identity of adult educators (Chapter Eight) and the role of professional associations in adult education (Chapter Seven) are also examined. Chapter Eight summarizes the ways in which the authors have framed the political landscape of adult education, and ways of strategizing around the needs of the field.

As Bolman and Deal (1991) have so aptly pointed out in their work on organizational politics, "the elements of a revolution include . . . a period of rising expectations followed by disappointment of those expectations" (p. 231). Given their insight and the insights of all of the contributors here, it would appear that there is no time like the present. The chapters that follow present a compelling argument for the ever-growing need for a concerted, collective effort aimed at strategic planning, advocacy, and change making for the lives of adult learners and for adult educators.

The focus of this volume is on the importance of understanding both the macro- and microenvironments that influence the work of adult educators and the need for strategizing around the negotiation of these politics. As such, it is also about agency, praxis, and the need for development of a critical pedagogy (Shor, 1987, 1996). This expanded framework of the political is useful not only in examining material and symbolic conditions and their connections, but in revealing the roles that educators may play in reproducing these conditions and strategizing around ways to make change.

References

Adams, F. *Unearthing Seeds of Fire: The Idea of Highlander.* Winston-Salem, N.C.: John F. Blair Publishers. 1975.

Addams, J. *Twenty Years at Hull House.* New York: Lightyear Press, 1996.

Amstutz, D. "Adult Basic Education: Equipped for the Future or for Failure?" In V. Sheared and P. A. Sissel (eds.), *Making Space: Merging Theory and Practice in Adult Education.* New York: Bergin & Garvey, 2001.

Apple, M. *Education and Power.* (2nd ed.) New York: Routledge, 1995.

Aronowitz, S., and Giroux, H. *Education Still Under Siege.* (2nd ed.) New York: Bergin & Garvey, 1993.

Baird, I. C. "Education, Incarceration and the Marginalization of Women." In V. Sheared and P. A. Sissel (eds.), *Making Space: Merging Theory and Practice in Adult Education.* New York: Bergin & Garvey, 2001.

Ball, S. *The Micropolitics of the School: Towards a Theory of School Organization.* London: Methuen, 1987.

Beder, H. "Popular Education: An to Approach Educational Strategy for Community-Based Organizations." In P. A. Sissel (ed.), *A Community-Based Approach to Literacy Programs: Taking Learners' Lives into Account.* San Francisco: Jossey-Bass, 1996.

Blase, J. "Everyday Political Perspectives of Teachers Toward Students: The Dynamics of Diplomacy." In J. Blase (ed.), *The Politics of Life in Schools.* Thousand Oaks, Calif.: Sage, 1991a.

Blase, J. "The Micropolitical Orientation of Teachers Toward Closed School Principals." *Education and Urban Society,* 1991b, *23,* 356–378.

Bolman, L., and Deal, T. *Reframing Organizations: Artistry, Choice, and Leadership.* San Francisco: Jossey-Bass, 1991.

Bounous, R. "Teaching as Political Practice." In V. Sheared and P. A. Sissel (eds.), *Making Space: Merging Theory and Practice in Adult Education.* New York: Bergin & Garvey, 2001.

Brookfield, S. D. "The Concept of Critically Reflective Practice." In A. L. Wilson and E. R. Hayes (eds.), *Handbook of Adult and Continuing Education.* San Francisco: Jossey-Bass, 2000.

Cervero, R., and Wilson, A. *Planning Responsibly for Adult Education: A Guide to Negotiating Power and Interests.* San Francisco: Jossey-Bass, 1994.

Childs, M. "Between a Rock and a Hard Place: Confronting Who 'We' Are." In V. Sheared and P. A. Sissel (eds.), *Making Space: Merging Theory and Practice in Adult Education.* New York: Bergin & Garvey, 2001.

Coben, D. *Radical Heroes. Gramsci, Freire and the Politics of Adult Education.* New York: Garland, 1998.

Cuban, S., and Hayes, E. "Women in Family Literacy Programs: A Gendered Perspective." In P. A. Sissel (ed.), *A Community-Based Approach to Literacy Programs: Taking Learners' Lives into Account.* San Francisco: Jossey-Bass, 1996.

Cunningham, P. M. "Race, Gender, and Class, and the Practice of Adult Education in the United States." In P. Wangoola and F. Youngman (eds.), *Towards a Transformative Political Economy of Adult Education: Theoretical and Practical Challenges.* DeKalb: LEPS Press, Northern Illinois University, 1996.

Cunningham, P. M. "Foreword." In V. Sheared and P. A. Sissel (eds.), *Making Space: Merging Theory and Practice in Adult Education.* New York: Bergin & Garvey, 2001.

Deshler, D., and Grudens-Schuck, N. "The Politics of Knowledge Construction." In A. L. Wilson and E. R. Hayes (eds.), *Handbook of Adult and Continuing Education.* San Francisco: Jossey-Bass, 2000.

Ewert, D. M., and Grace, K. A. "Adult Education for Community Action." In A. L. Wilson and E. R. Hayes (eds.), *Handbook of Adult and Continuing Education.* San Francisco: Jossey-Bass, 2000.

Flannery, D. "Changing Dominant Understandings of Adults as Learners." In E. Hayes and S.A.J. Colin III (eds.), *Confronting Racism and Sexism.* San Francisco: Jossey-Bass, 1994.

Foucault, M. *Power and Knowledge: Selected Interviews and Other Writings, 1972–1977.* New York: Pantheon Books, 1980.

Freire, P. *Pedagogy of the Oppressed.* New York: Seabury Press, 1970.

Galbraith, M. *Education Through Community Organizations.* San Francisco: Jossey-Bass, 1990.

Garrick, J., and Solomon, N. "Technologies of Learning at Work: Disciplining the Self." In V. Sheared and P. A. Sissel (eds.), *Making Space: Merging Theory and Practice in Adult Education.* New York: Bergin & Garvey, 2001.

Ginsburg, M. "Given a Head Start, Should One Cooperate or Compete?" In P. A. Sissel, *Staff, Parents, and Politics in Head Start: A Case Study in Unequal Power, Knowledge and Material Resources.* Bristol, Pa.: Falmer Press, 2000.

Ginsburg, M. B., Kamat, S., Raghu, R., and Weaver, J. "Educators and Politics: Interpretations, Involvement, and Implications." In M. Ginsburg (ed.), *The Politics of Educators' Work and Lives.* New York: Garland, 1995.

Giroux, H. "Teacher Education and the Ideology of Social Control." In H. Giroux (ed.), *Ideology, Culture, and the Process of Schooling.* Philadelphia: Temple University Press, 1981.

Giroux, H. *Theory and Resistance in Education: A Pedagogy for the Opposition.* New York: Bergin & Garvey, 1983.

Grace, A. P. "Using Queer Cultural Studies to Transgress Adult Educational Space." In V. Sheared and P. A. Sissel (eds.), *Making Space: Merging Theory and Practice in Adult Education.* New York: Bergin & Garvey, 2001.

Hall, B. L. "Continuity in Adult Education and Political Struggle." *Convergence: An International Journal of Adult Education,* 1978, *11,* 8–16.

Harper, L. "By My Own Eyes: A Story of Learning and Culture." In V. Sheared and P. A. Sissel (eds.), *Making Space: Merging Theory and Practice in Adult Education.* New York: Bergin & Garvey, 2001.

Hart, M. *Working and Educating for Life: Feminist and International Perspectives on Adult Education.* New York: Routledge, 1992.

Hayes, E., and Colin III, S.A.J. (eds.). *Confronting Racism and Sexism.* San Francisco: Jossey-Bass, 1994.

Hayes, E., and Flannery, D. *Women as Learners: The Significance of Gender in Adult Learning.* San Francisco: Jossey-Bass, 2000.

Hoyle, E. *The Politics of School Management.* London: Hodder and Stoughton. 1986.

Iannaconne, L. *Educational Policy Systems.* Fort Lauderdale, Fla.: Nova University Press, 1975.

Iannaconne, L. "Micropolitics of Education." *Education and Urban Society,* 1991, *23,* 465–471.

Jarvis, P. *Adult Education and the State: Towards a Politics of Adult Education.* New York: Routledge, 1993.

Jeria, J. "The Political Economy of Adult Education: Implications for Practice." In V. Sheared and P. A. Sissel (eds.), *Making Space: Merging Theory and Practice in Adult Education.* New York: Bergin & Garvey, 2001.

Johnson-Bailey, J., and Cervero, R. M. "An Analysis of the Educational Narratives of Reentry Black Women." *Adult Education Quarterly,* 1996, *46,* 142–157.

Johnson-Bailey, J., and Cervero, R. M. "The Invisible Politics of Race in Adult Education." In A. L. Wilson and E. R. Hayes (eds.), *Handbook of Adult and Continuing Education.* San Francisco: Jossey-Bass, 2000.

Kasworm, C., Sandmann, L., and Sissel, P. "Adults in Higher Education." In A. L. Wilson and E. R. Hayes (eds.), *Handbook of Adult and Continuing Education.* San Francisco: Jossey-Bass, 2000.

Knowles, M. *The Modern Practice of Adult Education.* New York: Association Press, 1970.

Kreisberg, S. *Transforming Power: Domination, Empowerment, and Education.* Albany: State University of New York Press, 1992.

Kreitlow, B. W. (ed.). *Examining Controversies in Adult Education.* San Francisco: Jossey-Bass, 1981.

Marshall, C., and Scribner, J. D. "It's All Political: Inquiry into the Micropolitics of Education." *Education and Urban Society,* 1991, *23,* 396–415.

Merriam, S. B. (ed.). *Selected Writings on Philosophy and Adult Education.* (2nd ed.) Melbourne, Fla.: Kreiger Publishing Co., 1995.

Quigley, A. *Rethinking Literacy Education: The Critical Need for Practice-Based Change.* San Francisco: Jossey-Bass, 1994.

Rist, R. "Student Social Class and Teacher Expectations: The Self-Fulfilling Prophecy in Ghetto Education." *Harvard Educational Review,* 1970, *40,* 411–451.

Rocco, T., and West, G. "Deconstructing Privilege: An Examination of Privilege in Education." *Adult Education Quarterly,* 1998, *48,* 171–184.

Sacks, P. *Generation X Goes to College: An Eye-Opening Account of Teaching in Postmodern America.* Chicago: Open Court, 1996.

Sheared, V. "Giving Voice: An Inclusive Model for Instruction—A Womanist Perspective." In E. Hayes and S.A.J. Colin III (eds.), *Confronting Racism and Sexism.* San Francisco: Jossey-Bass, 1994.

Sheared, V., and Sissel, P. A. "What Does Research, Resistance, and Inclusion Mean for Adult Education Practice?—A Reflective Response." In V. Sheared and P. A. Sissel (eds.), *Making Space: Merging Theory and Practice in Adult Education.* New York: Bergin & Garvey, 2001.

Shor, I. *Freire for the Classroom: A Sourcebook for Liberatory Teaching.* Portsmouth, N.H.: Boynton/Cook, 1987.

Shor, I. *When Students Have Power: Negotiating Authority in a Critical Pedagogy.* Chicago: University of Chicago Press, 1996.

Sissel, P. A. "Participation and Learning in Project Head Start: A Sociopolitical Analysis." *Adult Education Quarterly,* 1997, 47, 123–139.

Sissel, P. A. *Staff, Parents, and Politics in Head Start: A Case Study in Unequal Power, Knowledge and Material Resources.* Bristol, Pa.: Falmer Press, 2000.

Sissel, P. A., Birdsong, M. A., and Silaski, B. A. "A Room of One's Own: A Phenomenological Investigation of Class, Age, Gender, and Politics of Institutional Change Regarding Adult Students on Campus." In R. Nolan (ed.), *Proceedings of the 38th Annual Adult Education Research Conference.* Stillwater: Oklahoma State University, 1997.

Sissel, P. A., and Hohn, M. D. "Literacy and Health Communities: Potential Partners in Practice." In P. A. Sissel (ed.), *A Community-Based Approach to Literacy Programs: Taking Learners' Lives into Account.* San Francisco: Jossey-Bass, 1996.

Sissel, P. A., and Sheared, V. "Opening the Gates: Reflections on Power, Hegemony, Language, and the Status Quo." In V. Sheared and P. A. Sissel (eds.), *Making Space: Merging Theory and Practice in Adult Education.* New York: Bergin & Garvey, 2001.

Tisdell, E. "Interlocking Systems of Power, Privilege, and Oppression in Adult Higher Education Classes." *Adult Education Quarterly,* 1993, 43, 203–226.

Tisdell, E. J., and Taylor, E. W. "Adult Education Philosophy Informs Practice." *Adult Learning,* 2001, 11, 6–10.

Wagschal, K. "I Became Clueless Teaching the GenXers: Redefining the Profile of the Adult Learner." *Adult Learning,* 1997, 8, 21–25.

Wangoola, P., and Youngman, F. (eds.). *Towards a Transformative Political Economy of Adult Education: Theoretical and Practical Challenges.* DeKalb: LEPS Press, Northern Illinois University, 1996.

West, G., and Blumberg, R. L. "Reconstructing Social Protest from a Feminist Perspective." In G. West and R. L. Blumberg (eds.), *Women and Social Protest.* New York: Oxford University Press, 1990.

Willis, P. *Learning to Labor: How Working Class Kids Get Working Class Jobs.* New York: Columbia University Press, 1981.

Zinn, L. *Philosophy of Adult Education Inventory.* Boulder, Colo.: Lifelong Learning Options, 1999.

PEGGY A. SISSEL is a researcher and consultant with the Center for Applied Studies in Education at the University of Arkansas at Little Rock.

2

We challenge the broader adult education community to examine how they are either accommodating or reproducing hegemonic campus policies toward adult learners, take action to resist these policies, and support the development of improved policies, procedures, programs, and practices aimed toward adult learners in higher education.

The Politics of Neglect: Adult Learners in Higher Education

Peggy A. Sissel, Catherine A. Hansman, Carol E. Kasworm

Twenty years ago, K. Patricia Cross's book *Adults as Learners* (1981) alerted higher education to the growing presence of adults on college and university campuses. In doing so, she advocated for the development of a better understanding of the dispositional, situational, and institutional barriers that precluded adults from participating in learning within this setting and others.

Despite Cross's recommendation, few scholars have pursued sustained research on adults as learners within higher education. This dearth of scholarship is particularly noteworthy given the numbers of adults who have pursued postsecondary learning in the past thirty years. Between 1970 and 1991, enrollment of adults in credit-bearing classes grew by 171 percent (National Center for Education Statistics, 1995), and today, adults at many institutions are now the majority of degree-seeking students (College Board, 1998). A recent study by the College Board (1998) indicated that half of all students enrolled for credit within a U.S. college or university are over the age of twenty-five. When this population is added to those adults who participate in noncredit, extension, or college- or university-sponsored community and economic development initiatives, it becomes apparent that adult learners are the new majority in higher education (Kasworm, Sandmann, and Sissel, 2000).

Yet the experiences of adult learners in higher education and their learning needs, interests, and styles have largely been neglected (Schlossberg, Lynch, and Chickering, 1989; Kasworm, 1993; Kasworm, Sandmann, and Sissel, 2000). Some institutions are responsive to adult learners

(Council for Adult Experiential Learning, 2000), but neglect of adult learners in terms of public policy, programming, and mission can be found throughout higher education (Commission for a Nation of Lifelong Learners, 1997; Kasworm, Sandmann, and Sissel, 2000). As a result, adults are often institutionally invisible, marginalized, and taken for granted (Sissel, Birdsong, and Silaski, 1997), viewed as at-risk burdens or cash-cow boons (Richardson and King, 1998), or systematically ignored by the field of higher education (Sissel, 2001).

The political framework of analysis in this chapter develops connections between the social relations of the neglect of adult learners in higher education and the way in which material, cultural, and symbolic resources intersect with those relations through avenues of power and privilege. Our goal is to raise questions about the lack of privilege of adult learners and the reality of too few resources for adult learners on campuses and to posit ways of challenging reified youth-oriented ideologies and hegemonic practices through concrete acts of resistance. Approaching these issues from both an experiential and empirical perspective, we take a critical stance that both honors the experiences of adult learners in higher education and challenges our own roles as adult educators and advocates in higher education.

The Lack of Privilege in the Adult Student Experience

> When those who have the power to name and to socially construct reality choose not to see you or hear you, whether you are dark-skinned, old, disabled, female, or speak with a different accent than theirs, when someone with the authority of a teacher, say, describes the world and you are not in it, there is a moment of psychic disequilibrium, as if you looked into a mirror and saw nothing [Adrienne Rich, cited in Maher and Tetreault, 1994, p. 1].

Higher education is an elitist environment. Although many colleges and programs claim egalitarian ideals and suggest open access and support of all students, few institutions provide an even playing field, much less a nurturing environment for all. Because higher education has been anchored in its historical traditions of residential, selective education and because it is based in perceptions of a privileged place and role for young adult leadership development, this environment embraces full-time, residential youth. Little space, voice, and value are given to other groups and in particular those who are the most different from young students: adult learners. Adult students are often viewed as invisible and of lesser importance to the traditional core student group, as evidenced by higher education mission statements, publicity and image, and exclusion of adult requirements in the shaping of policies, programs, and outreach. Whether it is policy, program, attitudes, classroom environment, or funding support, adult learners face institutional neglect, prejudice, and denial of opportunities. Sissel, Birdsong, and Silaski (1997) have argued that this constellation of factors within institutions socially constructs adults as a class of learners in the academy. As a class, they are bound by multiple and overlapping political, cultural, educational, and informational characteristics that keep them at the margin, with little visibility or voice, and hence, no status, power, or privilege.

Scholars in various fields have addressed the notion of privilege and its importance in framing political questions. McIntosh's (1988) feminist theorization of white male privilege has been informative for its analysis of the symbiotic nature of the power-privilege dynamic within broad societal frameworks. Ball's (1987) work on the micropolitics of educational institutions connects the acquisition and distribution of resources, the development of relationships, and patterns of influence to the expressions of power in educational settings.

Sheared (1994) makes a direct link between marginality and the lack of power and privilege in adult education. Sheared explicates the notion of privilege as being a form of power that emanates from those at the center of power and works to expand or limit both the psyche, through self and group identification, and the social, through that individual or group's scope of access and agency. Sheared and Sissel (2001) note that this privilege, and hence access to the power and resources that come with such privilege, is conveyed through a hegemonic system that explicitly includes some groups and individuals and excludes others. Those who are invited into the centers of power are considered deserving or worthy, and those who are excluded are the "other." These others are constructed as such as a result of racism, classism, sexism, ageism, homophobia, or other "-isms" that function in our society as a means of separating us from each other, thereby keeping those in the margins powerless and voiceless.

Quinnan's (1997) critique of the status of adults in higher education focuses on the complicit relationship between the institutions of higher education and capitalism. His work deconstructs the adult normative role as worker, breadwinner, and functionary in a capitalist economy and juxtaposes it to that as learner. He argues that adults' lack of privilege stems from the emphasis in higher education on developing youth as future workers. By repressing adult visibility and access to learning, higher education keeps adults in the labor market, not in school.

The notion of privilege, then, is intimately connected to visibility and centrality, and privilege is bestowed through systems of power. One reflection of this lack of privilege is that adult students are often labeled with special words, such as *nontraditional, commuter,* or *reentry.* These labels define them as other, as marginal, and as needy in this college environment (Kasworm, 1993). Although the labels often are easy categories for separating adult students from traditional-aged college students, they do not provide respect and dignity for adult student qualities.

Some observers may dismiss such labels as mere descriptors, but in fact, such language is political, not only because of the lack of privilege it may signify but because labels on learners affect expectations and influence the actions of educators. As Rist (1970, 1972) and others (Good and Brophy, 1971; Rubovits and Maehr, 1973; U.S. Commission on Civil Rights, 1973; Persell, 1976; Tisdell, 1993; Sadker and Sadker, 1994; Swadener and Lubeck, 1995) have explicated, the expectations of educators are political. The view that educators hold about students affects how and what they teach, to whom, and whether they privilege students' life experiences, perspectives, and participation or work to diminish those insights and efforts.

Fraser (1989), in writing about the way in which dominant groups express power by reinterpreting the lived experiences of those who are marginalized, has pointed out that "dominant groups articulate need interpretations which are intended to exclude, defuse, and/or co-opt" (p. 166). She also notes that such counter-interpretations are political, explaining that "a matter is political if it is contested across a range of different discursive arenas and among a range of different discourse publics" (p. 167). The needs of adults are typically reinterpreted by those with power when they are expected to fit into policies, programs, and practices designed for full-time students between the ages of eighteen and twenty-two. In addition, adults are often perceived to have less academic competence, and although research indicates this typically is not the case (Kasworm and Pike, 1994; Darkenwald and Novak, 1997), admissions procedures, academic policies based in a youth-oriented schooling frame, and curricular and faculty access nevertheless position them as such.

The voice and image of adult students are not integrated into the ethos of the campus. Most collegiate institutions do not view their student population as older, married, and working. Whether it is admissions information, Web page discussions, or catalogue descriptions, adult students are not part of the descriptive landscape published by higher education institutions. Finally, most institutions have not accommodated and redefined themselves through their adult students. Because adults often represent evening, weekend, and distance learners, they are often denied full access and support, by both design and default. Most college campuses work on the assumption of a captured audience targeted to residential youth lifestyles. Many institutions make the assumption that students are able to transact business and engage in key learning experiences by coming to campus during the hours of 8 A.M. and 5 P.M. on weekdays, something not always possible for full-time working adults. Colleges and universities also often assume that they are interacting with youth in transition to adulthood; thus, attitudes and behaviors of administrators, support staff, and faculty, as well as policies and procedures of these institutions, are frequently condescending to adult students and do not take into account adult lifestyles and adult life complexities. There are often assumptions of communication between the campus and students through on-campus student newspapers and organizations. However, adults rarely seek out campus newspapers and rarely hear about on-campus events through other mechanisms. Of greater consequence is that institutions target most of their specialized resources toward daytime youth. This includes curricula offerings, honors opportunities, scholarships, key cocurricular events, and services such as career counseling. Such key resources do not support the growth, development, and well-being of adult learners.

Thus, in the context of higher education, privilege is constructed around notions of youth and is conveyed by a system of local, state, and federal policies, institution-specific programs, and professional practices. In a recent critique of higher education's policies, practices, and programs, Kasworm, Sandmann, and Sissel (2000) critically examine the myriad ways in which the needs, norms, and experiences of the eighteen- to twenty-two-year-old learners are systematically privileged within this system. This fixation on youth is particularly autocratic given that historically, two of the hallmarks of higher education policy in the United States centered around the learning needs of adults: the enactment of the Morrill Act's creation of land grant universities in 1862 and the GI Bill in 1944. Thus, although new federal legislation may be essential to making change, policymaking alone cannot, and will not, be the sole mechanism by which the youth-oriented hegemonic structure of U.S. higher education will be recreated into a system that meets the needs of learners of all ages.

The Politics of Resources and Advocacy

Advocates for adult learners must be politically savvy about higher educational policies, power, and privilege while having an awareness of the politics within the higher educational institution. Kanter (cited in Cervero and Wilson, 2001) describes politics as "the ability to get things done, to mobilize resources, to get and use whatever it is that a person needs for the goals he or she is attempting to meet" (p. 6). In other words, "politics is about who gets what, when, and how" (Osborne, cited in Ginsburg, Kamat, Raghu, and Weaver, 1995, p. 6). To get things done, one must be an advocate for equitable resources and just mechanisms of access. Therefore, educators must explicitly consider issues of power and domination, for only then can education help the powerless overcome the hegemonic structures that keep their voices, their needs, and their very presence marginalized (Giroux and Freire, 1987).

Marginalized is a term that can describe not only adult learners but the programs in place for them and their advocates in higher education. Services, programs, and policies for adults typically occur as peripheral add-ons, operating as exceptions to the mainstream programs for traditional students. Adults are often perceived as auxiliary enterprises, beyond the main endowed educational functions of the institution, and adult services and programs are often funded at a minimal level. In certain institutions, adult services and programs are based in a direct cost support from adult student fees, to the exclusion of institutional support.

Academic programs may marginalize adult learners further. Many adult academic programs are located in divisions of continuing education that offer more permeable boundaries and salient missions for adults. Unless these programs have a full complement of support services, however, adult students often find themselves in a schizoid pattern of attempting to accommodate and negotiate among competing traditional academic and continuing-education systems. For example, certain services may be offered to the evening school, and other policies and functions may be with the daytime academic programs. Other examples are adult-oriented programs and services that are hidden from immediate identification, buried within broad and complex academic units or hidden within traditional campus services as specialized options. These varied constructions of the academic environment represent the fragmentation and the limitations of place and privilege of adult learners.

Adult learners are typically served through student services personnel who are not in key power and advocacy roles. In addition, as supporters and promoters on campus for adult learners, advocates for adults can find themselves marginalized because of the very population they serve. This marginalization can manifest itself in poor salaries, scant resources, and small or nonexistent support staff to help accomplish programs. Program budgets may be so small that it becomes impossible financially and physically to offer even the most basic support programs for adult learners. In addition, offices or physical spaces that support adults may be hidden and hard to find. This lack of visibility is not entirely accidental; what is not seen will have no place to participate in power and privilege on campuses.

Advocates and adult students need to view the current social constructions of higher education reality while visioning different frameworks and assumptions to construct change and action. For both adult students and professionals who care about serving adults, there is need to delineate the key assumptions that frame the collegiate environment and have created disjuncture with adult student lives. Existing adult support services must be assessed in relation to the reality of the macrocollegiate environment (Kasworm, 1997). But change requires more than assessing current support services; it requires political awareness of the privilege and power on campus and the willingness to challenge current conditions while proposing and implementing better resources for adult learners.

The Politics of Positionality

The time is long past to reflect on the way in which we may be accommodating or reproducing the neglect of adult learners in our own locale and then to take action in resistance. To paraphrase McIntosh (1988), we must first unpack the meaning and measure of the privilege that we and our institutions give some students and not others and then act strategically.

According to Ginsburg, Kamat, Raghu, and Weaver (1995), every act, or omission, of teaching, research, and advocacy around the needs of students is political. If we as educators, advocates, and learners acknowledge this reality as it relates to adults in higher education, then how we act, or not act, with them and for them matters. In Chapter Seven in this volume, Cunningham reminds readers of the old adage that all politics is local. Similarly, feminists of the 1970s situated their call to action by framing the personal as political. These phrases are particularly applicable to politics in higher education because the scope, mission, and market of many higher education institutions are framed by regional, state, and local mandates and priorities. Cervero and Wilson (2001) argue that "adult education is not practiced on a neutral stage. . . . It happens in a social location that is defined by a particular social vision in relation to the wider systems of social, economic, and cultural relations to power" (p. 6). Thus, the way in which colleges and universities intersect with communities is both social and deeply personal; what occurs within and without the bounds of the ivory tower affects not only economies and communities but individuals and families.

If we position adult learners' experience in local terms, some of the essential questions regarding what higher education for adults in a particular locale looks like begin to emerge, including issues of access, information, curricula, support, and visibility. Interestingly, as Sissel, Birdsong, and Silaski (1997) point out, the posing of such questions may be threatening to higher education institutions that have not previously examined the experiences of adult learners. Since data collection about adult learners and the range of adult learning opportunities in higher education is not required by state and federal policies and is not systematically collected (Kasworm, Sandmann and Sissel, 2000), local institutions are unlikely to have it available. Thus, this simple act of questioning becomes a political act that exposes the structured invisibility of adults. Such visibility is critical; the work of resisting and contesting unequal distribution of resources will be fruitless until the need for change is recognized.

It is only when we link the silence and invisibility of adult learners to the politics of knowledge construction (Deshler and Grudens-Schuck, 2000) that we as adult educators begin to work to change those relations. Such change must begin with us, for it is not likely to occur within the field of higher education soon. The silence and invisibility of adult learners in higher education is so pervasive that with rare exception (Schlossberg, Lynch, and Chickering, 1989), the professional preparation of higher education administrators and student affairs professionals does not include information about adults as learners (Sissel, 2000). Thus, both the call for and the actual development of knowledge and information about adult learners in higher education must first come from outside the bounds of the traditional higher education research establishment.

Furthermore, as Sissel, Birdsong, and Silaski (1997) and the previous section indicate, this effort cannot be left solely to adult student campus advocates, for no matter how committed they are, their work and roles are as just as marginal as the students they serve. Still, the broader adult education community—the practitioners, scholars, and administrators who work in all programs related to adult learning—can support their work and increase the visibility of adults in higher education.

Professors of adult education and administrators of continuing-education and other programs within higher education institutions are system insiders who can begin to play an active role in raising questions about institutional policies, procedures, programs, practices, and data collection processes as they relate to adult learners. Yet in recent interviews with campus-based advocates for undergraduate adult learners, few connections among student services, professors, and continuing-education administrators were reported (Sissel, 2000).

Adult educators outside the system of higher education can also be invaluable voices for adult learners on campuses. Educators in community development, social service, and nonprofit organizations all work with adults who may have higher education aspirations. As leaders in the area of health and human services, the arts, religion, civic participation, professional groups, and other nonprofit groups, these adult educators are well positioned to raise questions about how higher education institutions are responding to the range of adult learning needs in communities. They can also advocate for the development of partnerships that place credit and non-credit opportunities in the heart of the community rather than behind campus walls.

Similarly, teachers and administrators in community-based and public school adult basic education and English as a Second Language programs can also work to develop a voice that breaks the silence about adult learners. Through the development of close connections with community and technical colleges, teachers can assist two-year institutions in developing a better understanding of the adult population in the community and their learning needs. Educators in adult high school and general equivalency diploma programs based in community colleges can act as advocates for adults, as can all instructors and administrators in community colleges. Such advocacy may lead to the development of articulation agreements with four-year institutions while also assisting higher education with information about and understanding of the adult population. Because community colleges are a valuable source of transfer students to colleges and universities, educators in the two-year colleges have the potential to play an important and economically powerful role by recommending that students transfer only to institutions that are adult friendly. From this perspective, educators in the military can also play this powerful mediating role, providing adults desiring to pursue higher education with vital information about institutions that place them at either the center or the margin.

Other sectors of the community can play a potent role in advocating for higher education's responsiveness to adults. The corporate and government sectors, each preoccupied with labor force needs and economic development, have strong interests in ensuring that higher education is responsive to community needs. Adult educators in those settings can assist higher education institutions in conceptualizing labor and economic development as an adult enterprise that engages a disparate and diverse population rather than framing such discussions around a homogeneous view of learners. Some efforts at program development and partnerships between these two sectors and higher education have helped create strong advocates within higher education (Coor, 1998).

Clearly, the experience of adults in higher education cannot be separated from politics, culture, economics, and social structures. Higher education culture and history have positioned adults as not being worthy of study, and few critical questions have been posed of higher education as it relates to adults. The act of questioning, when developed from a critical theory perspective, has implications for increased access and opportunity for individuals and greater visibility and understanding of the needs of all learners. Ultimately, such advocacy could lead to an enhanced community life grounded in democratic principles for all of us.

Conclusion

At the heart of all the concerns developed in this chapter has been the nature of positionality, the kind of metaknowledge that locates and mediates adult students in relation to others within the social structure. Adult students do live on the borderlands. They are not viewed as having a key position within higher education; rather, they are believed to be apart from this collegiate world of young adult development. They are often judged to be fragmented learners who cannot devote sufficient time, energy, and resources to intellectual engagement. Their environment of valuing family, work, and engagement in the community is not central to the collegiate relationship of students and of most higher education. They are judged to be other, to be less than the standard, and to be of limited potency related to the impact of a higher education.

The challenge of developing privilege and position for adult learners is to recognize the past and the future. Higher education has become a true marketplace not only of ideas, but also of options based on one's lineage and current status, as well as one's financial strength. To create a privileged space for adult learners, we need institutions that promote leadership for all learners. This means developing new understandings of adult life, adult work, and the adult place in civic responsibility and aligning that valued role with adults' role as learners in higher education. When these actions occur, adult access, support, and learning experiences will be enriched and no longer be hidden and fragmentary. As Maher and Tetrault (1994) contend, when we come to see and "understand the workings of positional dynamics in their lives, to see them through their 'third eye,' then they can begin to challenge them and to create change" (p. 203).

References

Ball, S. *The Micropolitics of the School: Towards a Theory of School Organization*. London: Methuen, 1987.

Cervero, R. M., and Wilson, A. L. "At the Heart of Practice: The Struggle for Knowledge and Power." In R. M. Cervero and A. L. Wilson (eds.), *Power in Practice: Adult Education and the Struggle for Knowledge and Power in Society*. San Francisco: Jossey-Bass, 2001.

College Board. *Adult Learning in America: Why and How Adults Go Back to School*. New York: College Board Publications, 1998.

Commission for a Nation of Lifelong Learners. *A Nation Learning: Vision for the 21st Century*. Albany, N.Y.: Regents College, 1997.

Coor, L. "Academic Values and Traditions." Plenary address at the Second Harvill Conference on Higher Education, Tucson, Ariz., Nov. 9, 1998.

Council for Adult Experiential Learning. *Best Practices in Adult Learning: A CAEL/APQC Benchmarking Study*. Chicago: Council for Adult Experiential Learning, 2000.

Cross, K. P. *Adults as Learners*. San Francisco: Jossey-Bass, 1981.

Darkenwald, G. G., and Novak, R. J. "Classroom Age Composition and Academic Achievement in College." *Adult Education Quarterly*, 1997, 47, 108–116.

Deshler, D., and Grudens-Schuck, N. "The Politics of Knowledge Construction." In A. L. Wilson and E. R. Hayes (eds.), *Handbook of Adult and Continuing Education*. San Francisco: Jossey-Bass, 2000.

Fraser, N. *Unruly Practices: Power, Discourse, and Gender in Contemporary Social Theory*. Minneapolis: University of Minnesota Press, 1989.

Ginsburg, M. B., Kamat, S., Raghu, R., and Weaver, J. "Educators and Politics: Interpretations, Involvement, and Implications." In M. Ginsburg (ed.), *The Politics of Educators' Work and Lives*. New York: Garland, 1995.

Giroux, H., and Freire, P. "Series Introduction." In D. W. Livingstone (ed.), *Critical Pedagogy and Cultural Power*. New York: Bergin & Garvey, 1987.

Good, T. L., and Brophy, J. E. "Analyzing Classroom Interaction: A More Powerful Alternative." *Educational Technology*, 1971, 11, 36–41.

Kasworm C. "An Alternative Perspective on Empowerment of Adult Undergraduates." *Contemporary Education*, 1993, 64, 162–165.

Kasworm, C. "Elitist Boundaries and the Impact of Privilege: Adult Higher Education Research and Policy." In P. Armstrong, N. Miller, and M. Zukas (eds.), *Crossing Borders, Breaking Boundaries: Research in the Education of Adults: An International Conference*. London: University of Birkbeck, July 1997.

Kasworm, C., and Pike, G. "Adult Undergraduate Students: Evaluating the Appropriateness of a Traditional Model of Academic Performance." *Research in Higher Education*, 1994, 35, 689–710.

Kasworm, C., Sandmann, L., and Sissel, P. "Adults in Higher Education." In A. L. Wilson and E. R. Hayes (eds.), *Handbook of Adult and Continuing Education*. San Francisco: Jossey-Bass, 2000.

Maher, F. A., and Tetreault, M.K.T. *The Feminist Classroom*. New York: Basic Books, 1994.

McIntosh, P. *White Privilege and Male Privilege: A Personal Account of Coming to See Correspondences Through Work in Women's Studies*. Wellesley, Mass.: Center for Research on Women, Wellesley College, 1988.

National Center for Education Statistics. *Profile of Older Undergraduates: 1989–90*. Washington, D.C.: U.S. Department of Education, Office of Educational Research and Improvement, 1995.

Persell, C. H. "Testing, Tracking, and Teachers' Expectations: Their Implications for Education and Equality. A Literature Review and Synthesis." Unpublished report, 1976. (ED 126 150.)

Quinnan, T. W. *Adult Students "at Risk": Culture Bias in Higher Education*. New York: Bergin & Garvey, 1997.

Richardson, J., and King, E. "Adult Students in Higher Education: Burden or Boon?" *Journal of Higher Education*, 1998, *69*, 65–88.
Rist, R. "Student Social Class and Teacher Expectations: The Self-Fulfilling Prophecy in Ghetto Education." *Harvard Educational Review*, 1970, *40*, 411–451.
Rist, R. "Social Distance and Social Inequality in a Ghetto Kindergarten Classroom." *Urban Education*, 1972, *7*, 241–260.
Rubovits, P. C., and Maehr, M. "Pygmalion Black and White." *Journal of Personality and Social Psychology*, 1973, *25*, 210–218.
Sadker, M., and Sadker, D. *Failing at Fairness: How America's Schools Cheat Girls.* Old Tappan, N.J.: Macmillan, 1994.
Schlossberg, N. K., Lynch, A. Q., and Chickering, A. W. *Improving Higher Education Environments for Adults: Responsive Programs and Services from Entry to Departure.* San Francisco: Jossey-Bass, 1989.
Sheared, V. "Giving Voice: A Womanist Construction." In E. Hayes and S.A.J. Colin III (eds.), *Confronting Racism and Sexism in Adult Continuing Education.* San Francisco: Jossey-Bass, 1994.
Sheared, V., and Sissel, P. A. "What Does Research, Resistance, and Inclusion Mean for Adult Education Practice?—A Reflective Response." In V. Sheared and P. Sissel (eds.), *Making Space: Merging Theory and Practice in Adult Education.* New York: Bergin & Garvey, 2001.
Sissel, P. A. "When 'Accommodation' Is Resistance: Towards a Critical Discourse on the Politics of Adult Education." In R. M. Cervero, B. C. Courtenay, and C. H. Monagham (eds.), *The Cyril O. Houle Scholars in Adult and Continuing Education Global Research Perspectives.* Athens: University of Georgia, 2001.
Sissel, P. A., Birdsong, M. A., and Silaski, B. A. "A Room of One's Own: A Phenomenological Investigation of Class, Age, Gender, and Politics of Institutional Change Regarding Adult Students on Campus." In R. Nolan (ed.), *Proceedings of the 38th Annual Adult Education Research Conference.* Stillwater: Oklahoma State University, 1997.
Swadener, B., and Lubeck, S. *Children and Families at Promise: Deconstructing the Discourse of Risk.* Albany: State University of New York Press, 1995.
Tisdell, E. J. "Interlocking Systems of Power, Privilege, and Oppression in Adult Higher Education Classes." *Adult Education Quarterly*, 1993, *43*, 203–226.
U.S. Commission on Civil Rights. *Teachers and Students: Differences in Teacher Interaction with Mexican American and Anglo Students. Report V: Mexican American Study.* Washington, D.C.: U.S. Government Printing Office, 1973.

PEGGY A. SISSEL is a researcher and consultant with the Center for Applied Studies in Education at the University of Arkansas at Little Rock.

CATHERINE A. HANSMAN is associate professor and program director of the M.Ed. program in adult learning and development and the leadership and lifelong learning track in the Ph.D. program in urban education at Cleveland State University, Ohio.

CAROL E. KASWORM is department chair and professor in the Department of Adult and Community College Education, North Carolina State University, Raleigh.

3

The authors reflect on their experiences incorporating democratic ideals in their work as university professors in an adult education doctoral program.

Negotiating the Democratic Classroom

Scipio A. J. Colin III, Thomas W. Heaney

> Much of what passes for adult education involves routine maintenance of reality in that the assumptions and objectives underlying many courses exist against the background of a world that is silently taken-for-granted . . . [and is] implicitly ideological in [its] maintenance of the institutionalized reality.
>
> D. O'Sullivan (1991, p. 224)

Making explicit the political dimensions of a graduate classroom can be a daunting and anxiety-producing task. It is daunting in that academic hierarchy and professorial authority appear to be unassailably permanent features of the university, impervious to political influence. It is anxiety producing in that any political gaze risks laying bare the contractions of an adult education practice within higher education, a practice that frequently—inevitably, it would seem—ignores the democratic ideals of the field.

Democracy and the University

Is democracy possible in the context of higher education? We argue that it is, recognizing that democracies always exist in the midst of contradictory and hegemonic institutions and thus are not totalizing structures. The options for democratic decision making and action have always been hedged by external constraints. Democracy, however conceived, is always circumscribed, limited by borders within which shared decision making and self-governance occur. In any democracy, some areas of concern are kept off the agenda for public discourse, and others are imposed by more powerful groups outside the borders. Some of these powerful outsider groups are also thought to be democracies.

Because the practice of democracy is always circumscribed within regimes of power, democracy requires constant vigilance. Hence, the challenge to create a participatory practice within the higher education classroom inevitably involves pushing the borders, anticipating and countering resistance. It is in engagement with this struggle that genuine participation and democracy are attained. In our efforts to construct a doctoral program around democratic practice, we frequently reflect on obstacles encountered rather than become bogged down in frustration and outrage. In hindsight, the obstacles we encountered prove to be the same as those encountered by any other group attempting to live democratically.

Inventing a Democratic Practice

We do not assume that everyone shares our understanding of what constitutes a democratic practice. For many, democracy means majority rule, a practice that by implication excludes minorities. Although some would argue that adult educators are inclusionary (after all, this ideal is embedded in our mission), both demographics and curricula clearly indicate that the political and participatory reality of our field contradicts inclusivity. Neither our knowledge base nor our academic environments reflect the racial or gender diversity of the larger society. Embedded in our literature is the principle of intellectual majority rule—that in truth and practice, we do not view all ideas, concepts, and theories as intellectual equals. Our view is more in line with *Webster's* (1991) definition of democracy as "the absence of hereditary arbitrary class distinctions or privileges" (p. 338).

In our view, however, democracy in education can occur only within a teaching-learning environment that provides opportunities for the articulation and analysis of multiple sociocultural experiences. Democratic practice takes us beyond cultural provincialism by confronting issues of intellectual imperialism and conceptual colonialism. Such a practice includes often excluded racial and gender groups in the discourse and environment of the classroom.

Regarding the issues of racial exclusion, specifically the Africentric paradigm, Colin (1994) argues that "our curriculum must incorporate knowledge that comes from outside the Eurocentric dominant cultural and ideological framework. By including this knowledge base (Africentrism), we make space for those current and potential research scholars who possess such knowledge and who have an Africentric perspective" (p. 59).

Harding's (1996) argument regarding gender exclusion is that "women's ways of knowing show how legitimating and exploring diversely socially situated knowledges can expand human knowledge while also advancing recognition of the richness and diversity of human cultural traditions. With such a culturally respectful epistemological program, advancing knowledge can be more firmly linked to advancing democratic social relations" (pp. 448–449).

We believe that democratic educational practice must by its nature and design confront intellectual censorship and challenge the false and ethnocentric universals of concepts, ideas, and theories. This position is clearly reflected in both what we teach—Africentric pedagogy, womanist consciousness, critical theory, and critical feminist pedagogy—and in who teaches, as reflected in the racial and gender composition of our faculty. Guy (1999) conceptualizes this approach as "cultural democracy," which "refers to the goal of living in a society in which multiplicity of cultures not only coexists but also thrives. From this perspective, monocultural norms and practices must be rejected in favor of a restructuring of cultural and social processes that are broadly inclusive. For adult educators this requires an examination of educational practices to make them culturally relevant to the needs and cultural backgrounds of learners" (pp. 13–14).

The Basis of Student Power

At its root, the development of a democratic practice is about balancing and negotiating power among groups that embody diverse cultural and gendered norms. The power and privilege associated with a Eurocentric, professorial class in a postsecondary classroom cannot be dismissed by a mere exercise of will or sublimated in an excess of democratic fervor. The inequities of race, gender, and class are deeply embedded in the institutional claims and functions of the university. It is the university's mission not only to disseminate knowledge but also to legitimize those who acquire it and fail those who have not met dominant norms. The power to name what it is that constitutes knowledge and to stand in judgment over those who seek to attain it is the ground and substance of professorial privilege.

While academic position and institutional authority vest faculty with day-to-day control over curriculum and the power of grading, the basis of student power is less clear. As with most other communities on the margins, the strength of students lies not in institutions or wealth but in their numbers. Once students begin to speak with one voice, their power is manifest.

In cohort-based learning, ongoing, long-term relationships develop among peers. The interests of learners, forged with the strength of numbers, demand that education be undertaken *by* and *with* students, not *to* them. Shor (1996) described this as the "democratic disturbance of the teacher-centered classroom" (p. 148). Individualized students, vulnerable in the face of faculty power, are often fearful of speaking critically or providing honest feedback. Students who find common cause and a forum for expressing their concerns are much more likely to challenge oppressive and dysfunctional classroom practices.

Democracy and Collaboration

In "Democracy and the Friendship Pattern," Lindeman wrote:

> The three slogans of the French Revolution, from which event so many of the values of American Democracy were derived, were Liberty, Equality and Fraternity. . . . Without equality, liberty becomes a form of dissociation. And without fraternity, equality is no more than a cold mechanical achievement. The essence of fraternity is friendship, and friendship can only develop among persons who see each other face-to-face, who exchange their common beliefs and their divergences, who share experiences [cited in Brookfield, 1987, p. 152].

In our practice, a cohort-based doctoral program in adult education, students and faculty share an intensive residential experience for two weeks each summer. During this institute, students are challenged to devise their own model of democracy—a structure by which they can identify the concerns of their peers, develop strategies for the resolution of these concerns, and subsequently negotiate these solutions with faculty. Students meet without faculty present until their concerns and strategies have been identified in order to avoid front-loading student decision making with professorial opinions.

Once students have agreed on a structure of governance, all student concerns, except for personal matters not affecting the cohort, are brought first to their governing body. Faculty no longer need to respond to suggestions of individuals who seek changes in the curriculum or in classroom procedures. Once changes are sought by the governance group, however, these suggestions demand careful consideration and action by faculty. Student governance provides ongoing formative evaluation and allows adjustments to emerging needs of learners. Governance also provides the experiential content for discussions of democracy, a core concept in our conceptualization of an adult education practice.

Democracy at the Core of Adult Education

Eduard Lindeman was one of the first to identify the emerging field of adult education in his seminal work, *The Meaning of Adult Education* (1989), first published in 1926. His visionary reflections on adult education were what many would identify as the self-conscious beginnings of adult education history in the United States. As Heaney (1996) noted:

> Grounded in the progressive and pragmatic tradition and building on the work of his colleague and friend, John Dewey, Lindeman observed the interdependence of an informed public and democracy—a relationship at the core of Dewey's philosophy of education—and expanded Dewey's notions about school-based edu-

cation for democratic participation to adults who throughout their lives struggled to participate in social and economic decisions affecting them [pp. 4–5].

For Lindeman, what distinguished adult education from other forms of education was the fact that its purpose is social and that it is integral to the democratic struggle (Brookfield, 1984). Adult education is an essential component of a democratic society. Its absence leaves decisions in the hands of an educated elite, promotes a cult of experts, and erodes democratic social order. Such a view reflected the spirit of the times, the spirit of possibility and confidence that inspired both grassroots learning and action exemplified in labor colleges, town hall meetings, the Chautauqua, and the Highlander Folk School.

Through various publications, we have articulated as a primary goal of our doctoral program the emergence of our graduates as change agents, committed to facilitating a shift in power within the context of their respective practices—a shift that will reconfigure societal relationships and result in a significant enhancement of the quality of life for those whom they serve.

Through our research agendas and teachings, we encourage the identification of complex relationships between and among various interest groups and analysis of the sociocultural factors of race, gender, and class. We, along with our research scholars, dissect and critique how and in what ways these factors shape and influence our perceptual patterns and subsequently our practice. Indeed, these are the salient issues that frame the critical discourse within the context of our teaching-learning environment (Colin, 1994; Heaney, 1996; Heaney and Strohschen, 2000; Tisdell, 2000).

For us, our conceptualization of what constitutes democratic practice is truly reflective of what we perceive the mission of the field to be. It is the implementation of a practice that begins with a sociocultural critique of conceptual shifts that occur as a result of critical discourse. It is a liberatory and transformative process that effects changes not only within our research scholars but also within ourselves.

It is within this framework that the doctoral program in adult education at National-Louis University was designed. In this program, the aim of adult education is conceptualized not as the acquisition of knowledge alone but as the acquisition of knowledge that strengthens the knower's sense of responsibility and influence over decisions that affect day-to-day life. Whether in the workplace or the community, adult learners are diminished not only by ignorance but also by powerlessness. At the core of adult education practice thus conceived is the practice of democracy—shared decision making in the face of an inequitable distribution of power.

Limits to Academic Democracy

The issue of power is widely discussed among both students and faculty. The governance process that each cohort of students has devised increasingly challenges faculty to involve learners more fully in developing the curriculum. As faculty, we try to respond positively, but inevitably we have found it difficult at times to let go of the prerogatives and privileges of our professorial position. At times, we have cloaked ourselves in a rationale of efficiency, arguing that logistics and timeliness are better served by a planning process that involves fewer people. We have argued from our lofty position of special knowledge that the "information" on which the curriculum is based is available to students only as the curriculum unfolds in course work. How do faculty and students share this information before the course begins—indeed, before the syllabus is prepared? And so many decisions are made without benefit of student consultation. Such preemptory decisions by faculty contradict the democratic principles of our classroom and can result in conflict.

In such moments of disagreement, we readily recognize the contextually complex environment that our graduate classroom presents for democracy. In fact, we have not one but several democracies working, sometimes in tandem but occasionally at cross-purposes. Ours is at minimum a tricameral structure in which each body has specific areas of responsibility.

The first democracy, the student governance group, struggles to build consensus among peers who frequently have divergent interests. The second democracy, the two or three members of the faculty team teaching in a term, struggles with collegiality in melding the content of several courses. And both groups—students and faculty—struggle to create democracy in their negotiations of day-to-day practice in the classroom. The third democratic structure, the doctoral steering committee, guides the whole enterprise, assessing the curriculum and applying policies set by the department and the university.

The practice of democracy is complicated by relationships among these three bodies, each with its own interests, requiring negotiation and compromise when in conflict. A limitation, but not a barrier, to the development of democratic decision making is the special responsibility of faculty for maintaining standards and policy in the context of an academic institution. The faculty are also accountable in some imprecise way to the field of study, causing them at times to assume the role of guardian of the boundaries of the field in resolving student-faculty differences—boundaries that maintain the hegemony of dominant (Euroameripean) norms. The university exerts its own demands on both faculty and students through a separate apparatus of faculty governance. All of this gets very messy. Working through issues requires patience, perseverance, and a willingness to question without pretending we can change everything.

A Tale of Two Countries

Nowhere does the tension between democracy and "standards" become clearer than in collaborative inquiry, and specifically in relation to the doctoral dissertation. In our program, this major research project is called a critical engagement project (CEP) in order to place emphasis on the ways in which the researcher will be engaged in not merely naming but transforming the world. No one should have greater commitment to or interest in the outcome of a CEP than the research scholar who undertakes the rigors of this task. We have found that most doctoral students hold themselves to the highest of standards, requiring little exercise of overt faculty power in order to ensure that the stringent requirements of academic research are met. Our research scholars are responsible for coordinating their own CEP teams, thus equivalently chairing their own dissertation committees. *Critical Engagement Project: A Manual* defines that core faculty will "determine when or whether a CEP is accepted in partial fulfillment of the requirements for graduation" (Heaney, 2000, p. 15). Nonetheless, the manual cautions students that "while the faculty can offer support and challenge at various points, you are the primary navigator of this adventure" (p. 4).

This process in which both the research scholar and faculty have voice is another instance of a persisting question: Is democracy consistent with the negotiation of matters in which one partner in the negotiation makes the ultimate decision? For example, after all the discussion and negotiation occur, it is faculty who decide whether a student's work is complete. Similarly, who makes the ultimate decision regarding a syllabus? Students have generally asked that faculty take responsibility for planning the first few days of each term and make proposals for subsequent blocks of time to which the students could respond and negotiate changes. The development of curriculum can involve both students and faculty in a democratic process. But at issue are institutional roles, expertise, and experience.

One of the students several years ago argued that the inequitable distribution of power in the higher education classroom led unavoidably to faculty domination. He projected the image of students as citizens of one democratic country and faculty as members of another. However, the Country of Faculty is the more powerful and assumes the role of protector over the Country of Student. The Country of Faculty is able to reject norms and standards developed by the citizens of Student, because Faculty did not have anything to do with their development. He asked, "What makes this different from colonialism?"

This challenging question goes beyond the issue of voice. The argument is not merely that students' voices must be heard, but that their voice should effect that which they name. While faculty can certainly develop the means by which the students are consulted in the syllabus-building process, responsibility for the final decision regarding such matters in the university rests with the faculty.

Learning to Be Free Democratically

From the frustrations and accomplishments of the past four years, we have learned many lessons. We agree with Manning's (1992) observation that "a political vision of emancipation is more than a set of ambitious goals, it's the courage to state what's wrong with our society. . . . The real problem isn't with the politicians; it's within ourselves" (p. 248). To assist those who would challenge the assumptions, ideas, and processes that perpetuate anti-democratic practices in our graduate programs, we offer the following suggestions:

• We must first practice what we teach. This means that we should have an articulated plan to transform ourselves through ongoing learning. This begins with the acknowledgment that what we may know about something is not all there is to be known. We must relentlessly search out other intellectual paradigms and make space for competing ideas, concepts, and philosophies.

• We must be willing to consider alternative models of graduate adult education. We would argue that only the cohort model allows for the consistency of time and space needed to create an environment conducive to democratic practice. The interrelationship of mutual trust, respect, and academic democratic practice is not one that can be developed within a single semester and maintained over the duration of a program.

• We must not be afraid to critique the assumptions that influence our social and political worldview. Clearly, these assumptions are not inalterable states of being. A heightened level of social consciousness will alter our view regarding the sociopolitical implications of our practice.

References

Brookfield, S. "The Contribution of Eduard Lindeman to the Development of Theory and Philosophy in Adult Education." *Adult Education Quarterly,* 1984, *34,* 185–196.

Brookfield, S. *Learning Democracy: Eduard Lindeman on Adult Education and Social Change.* London: Croom Helm, 1987.

Colin, S.A.J. III. "Adult and Continuing Education Graduate Programs: Prescription for the Future" In E. Hayes and S.A.J. Colin III (eds.), *Confronting Racism and Sexism.* New Directions for Adult and Continuing Education, no. 61. San Francisco: Jossey-Bass, 1994.

Guy, T. C. " Culture as Context for Adult Education: The Need for Culturally Relevant Adult Education." In T. C. Guy (ed.), *Providing Culturally Relevant Adult Education: A Challenge for the Twenty-First Century.* New Directions for Adult and Continuing Education, no. 82. San Francisco: Jossey-Bass, 1999.

Harding, S. "Gendered Ways of Knowing and the 'Epistemological Crisis' of the West." In N. Goldberger, J. Tarule, B. Clinchy, and M. Belenky (eds.), *Knowledge, Difference, and Power.* New York: Basic Books, 1996.

Heaney, T. *Adult Education for Social Change: From Center Stage to the Wings and Back Again.* Columbus, Ohio: Ohio State University, 1996.

Heaney, T. (ed.). *Critical Engagement Project: A Manual.* Chicago: National-Louis University, 2000.

Heaney, T., and Strohschen, G. " This Isn't Kansas Anymore, Toto." In M. S. Eisen and E. Tisdell (ed.), *Team Teaching and Learning in Adult Education Contexts.* New Directions for Adult and Continuing Education, no. 87. San Francisco: Jossey-Bass, 2000.

Lindeman, E. *The Meaning of Adult Education.* Norman, Okla.: University of Oklahoma, 1989. (Originally published 1926.)

Manning, M. "A Strategy for Democracy: Empowerment, Leadership and Vision." In M. Manning, *The Crisis of Color and Democracy: Essays on Race, Class and Power.* Monroe, Me.: Common Courage Press, 1992.

O'Sullivan, D. "Socialization, Social Change and Ideology in Adult Education." *Journal of Educational Thought/Revue de la Pensée Educative,* 1991, *25,* 222–227.

Shor, I. *When Students Have Power: Negotiating Authority in a Critical Pedagogy.* Chicago: University of Chicago Press, 1996.

Tisdell, E. "Feminist Pedagogies." In E. Hayes and D. Flannery (eds.), *Women as Learners.* San Francisco: Jossey-Bass, 2000.

Webster's Ninth New Collegiate Dictionary. Springfield, Mass.: Merriam-Webster, 1991.

SCIPIO A. J. COLIN III is an associate professor and chair of the Department of Adult and Continuing Education, National-Louis University, Chicago.

THOMAS W. HEANEY is an associate professor and director of the adult education doctoral program, Department of Adult and Continuing Education, National-Louis University, Chicago.

4

Finding a niche in teacher education programs in colleges of education can help adult educators secure their place in higher education while still maintaining integrity within the discipline.

Achieving Voice and Security in Colleges of Education

Michael J. Day, Donna D. Amstutz, Donna L. Whitson

Tension between idealism and realism in adult education and the place of each in higher education will probably never be fully resolved. Such tension may even be viewed as a positive element for the discipline of adult education, causing the field continually to clarify its purpose and reaffirm its philosophical beliefs about what adult educators do. Addressing such tension compels graduate programs in adult education to determine what they are and where they fit in the world, specifically in the world of higher education.

Historically, reality for many adult education programs in higher education has meant finding a niche in colleges of education. Not too surprisingly, educators of differing age groups and differing educational settings commonly disagree on the ideals that guide their practice. Because in education, as in art, literature, and philosophy, idealism is the educator's conception of perfection, differing ideals may, and indeed often do, result in tension.

In this chapter, we examine some elements of the tension between idealism and reality that exist for many adult education professors in institutions of higher education and share an approach that we have adopted for reducing this tension at our institution.

Seeds of Tension

During the more than seventy years of existence as an academic discipline in the United States, the field of adult education has spent a great deal of time examining itself as both an emerging and a distinct field of

NEW DIRECTIONS FOR ADULT AND CONTINUING EDUCATION, no. 91, Fall 2001   © John Wiley & Sons, Inc.

study. The emphasis has been to extend the legitimacy of education as a field of study beyond K–12 education, and central to this argument was the articulation of differences between adult educational practices and that of other educators, such as public school teachers. No chapter in the *Handbook of Adult Education in the United States* in 1934 (Rowden), 1936 (Rowden), 1948 (Ely), 1960 (Knowles), 1964 (Jensen, Liveright, and Hallenbeck), 1970 (Smith, Aker, and Kidd), or 1990 (Merriam and Cunningham) directly discussed similarities between adult education and K–12 education. The occasional mention of youth or public school adult education programs was framed with a focus on adult education as a separately run activity from K–12 education and was generally a comparison of how adult education differs from and is distinctly separate from K–12 education theory and practice. As Knowles (1970) was proposing andragogy as an alternative to pedagogy and as members of the professorate were investigating the "deschooled" society of Illich (1970), the distinction between adult education and K–12 education throughout the 1970s and 1980s was purposefully made.

Even a cursory glance at the dominant literature of the field over the past few decades, such as *Phi Delta Kappan, Adult Education Quarterly, Adult Learning, Change,* and Educational Resources Information Center publications, reveals the changing thoughts about education and learning. Ironically, while academic programs in adult education attempted to achieve legitimacy and support through distinction, an ever-increasing number of K–12 educators were embracing a learner-centered philosophy and espousing tenets of lifelong learning, ideals advocated by adult educators since the 1920s. In addition, both K–12 educators and adult educators were addressing the need for educational reform.

Finally, Peters and others (1991), while looking at the development of adult education as an academic field of study, hinted at problems that were beginning to appear nationally. From a Commission of Professors of Adult Education report issued in 1988, it was noted that nine threats to adult education programs currently existed; among them were isolation from other fields and disciplines and lack of commitment to other programs or departments with which adult educator were affiliated. Nevertheless, no discussion in this report addressed the merits of involving adult education faculty in K–12 teacher preparation programs as a rather natural evolution of a commitment to lifelong learning in schools of education.

It is little wonder that graduate programs in adult education continue to struggle. They are still striving to find their niche and establish their legitimacy within colleges of education. In the meantime, tensions continue to build. These tensions, both perceived and real, between college K–12 faculty and adult education faculty, stem from many sources. The five discussed here are beliefs about knowledge, schools, learning, and teaching, and resource allocation. These tensions are often the basis on which justification for lack of involvement in undergraduate programs exists.

Beliefs About Knowledge. Faculties' beliefs about knowledge define who and what they value in learning situations. A primary dissimilarity between adult education and K–12 faculty is related to views of knowledge. Adult educators often see knowledge as relative, transient, and constantly evolving (Hill, 1995; Hart, 1992; Freire, 1970) rather than as fixed. However, our experiences reveal that some K–12 faculty view knowledge as specific content that needs to be "taught" to the students in order to make them "knowledgeable." This view, promoted by Bloom (1987) and Hirsch (1988), prescribes cultural knowledge from a particular or dominant cultural tradition and views it as better or more important than knowledge from other traditions. The pervasiveness of this view, which is "objective" and "scientific," hides its true value-laden nature. That K–12 faculty members may view worthwhile knowledge as that which can be assessed by norm- or criterion-referenced tests is obvious from the nationwide proliferation of standardized testing and state accountability standards. From this framework of knowledge come the historical values of behavioral, individualistic, and cognitive knowledge.

Although there has been a recent emphasis on constructivism in many colleges of education, we have observed that not infrequently, K–12 faculty believe that a learner's role is passively to absorb subject matter content and knowledge that is generated by teachers. We, on the other hand, as adult education professors, generally encourage students to actively generate their own knowledge that may conflict with previously held beliefs about knowledge. These differing views of knowledge may create tension between K–12 and adult education faculty members.

Beliefs About Schools. K–12 faculty and administrators may view *education* and *schooling* as synonymous. Due to extensive involvement in elementary and secondary education that occurs almost exclusively in schools, educators outside the adult education framework commonly discuss education in the context of formal schooling. Adult educators, on the other hand, generally focus on learning that occurs outside the K–12 framework. In the practice of adult education, the learning process is seldom confined to specially constructed buildings; education also takes place in homes and communities. Thus, the false notion that adult education and K–12 education are completely separate systems may be created.

This distinction between separate K–12 and adult education domains is now being challenged. As more and more adults are pressed into formal continuing-education programs, adult education increasingly is framed by formal institutions, such as the military, other government agencies, and businesses where training is often mandated. Adults may resent being forced to learn and relearn tasks that others have defined for them and recognize that both training and schooling are institutionalized forms of learning. Thus, tension may exist not only between K–12 and adult education faculty but also between adult education faculty themselves regarding schooling. Some adult education professors emphasize human resource development, others emphasize adult basic education (both considered forms of schooling), and others emphasize the learning that takes place within the community but outside school settings, such as in programs sponsored by associations, clubs, libraries, and action groups.

Beliefs About Learning. In the 1960s and 1970s, adult education professors were often concerned with distinguishing the difference between adult educators and educators of children. Many of the major tenets that Knowles (1970) proposed attempted to define the ways in that adults learn differently from children. Although Knowles (1980) later modified his views somewhat regarding the assumptions surrounding the education of children compared with that of adults, he nevertheless still stressed differing assumptions about learning.

In addition, K–12 faculty and adult education faculty may differ in their use of learning objectives. Whereas K–12 faculty may specify beforehand what the learning outcome should be, adult education faculty may be more likely to emphasize learning outcomes that the learners themselves define as they progress through a learning process. The objectives may or may not be obvious before learning clarifies the need for a particular outcome. These different approaches to learning may also create tensions between adult education faculty and others in the college of education, contributing to the distancing of adult education and K–12 faculty.

Beliefs About Teaching. Since the 1920s, there has been almost a canonical reverence for adult educators as facilitators for learning as opposed to "sages on the stage." The Socratic method, the problem posing method proposed by Freire (1970), and the focus in the 1950s and 1960s on group processes in adult education contributed to this fervor. But in what ways is this view about teaching unique to adult education? K–12 faculty members have been using group processes in their classrooms for many years, probably since Dewey (1916) expounded on the virtues of helping students discover knowledge for themselves. While some elementary and secondary school faculty emphasize both cooperative and constructivist learning, which portray the teacher as a facilitator, undergraduate teacher preparation programs across the country generally continue to be teacher centered. That is, these programs tend to stress the teacher as expert, assigning to him or her the role of transmitter of knowledge. Because adult education professors often teach in ways that challenge the authority and ownership of knowledge of educators at all levels, they may push their students to question traditional ways of teaching. In response, K–12 faculty may accuse adult education faculty members of undermining their authority.

Adult educators may be able to provide support for K–12 faculty who emphasize student-centered, student-in-control environments in the public schools because adult education often has a student-centered focus. As adult educators, we commonly encourage the maturation of the student through the teaching-learning process and reaffirm that excellent teachers teach not the subject but the student; they employ the curriculum as a means to empower students and not as an end in and of itself. The tension created by these different beliefs about teaching may contribute to isolation of the adult education faculty from K–12 faculty.

Issues Surrounding Resource Allocation. Programs that focus only on graduate education are high cost for universities and time intensive for faculty members. Given the current climate in higher education that demands integration, accountability, and justification for all academic disciplines, adult education graduate programs are frequently asked to provide a rationale for their continued inclusion in colleges of education. Although often the argument centers on philosophic ideals, a business mentality has been imposed on many university administrative structures. It seems quite natural for K–12 faculty to see adult education faculty as taking limited resources. For example, as a president or provost looks for ways to respond to tightening economic constraints, adult education may be mentioned as not being integral to the mission of colleges of education. In higher administrative circles, adult education graduate programs often become a potential cost-saving area that could be cut without sacrificing what is considered to be the "real" college of education mission: to prepare elementary and secondary teachers. K–12 educators may mirror these administrative beliefs and may try to limit the mission of their college to teacher preparation and related areas such as school counseling and educational administration and leadership. On the other hand, based on our experiences, given an environment that often pushes faculty to generate additional dollars to support their graduate degree programs, adult education faculty may need to be entrepreneurial. Ironically, other faculty members who are often dealing with significant decreases in their own resources may resent any success in this area.

Resolving the Tension

Tension stemming from differing views regarding knowledge, schooling, learning, teaching, and resource allocation often exists. Based on the issues and information we have presented, adult education professors may react to these tensions from one of three perspectives. The purists may be unwilling to pursue anything less than perfection and remain adamant that there can be no compromise between their idealism and the K–12 worldview of other college of education faculty. For adult education professors in higher education who subscribe to this view, this stance may leave no options other than walking away from the situation by resigning their positions. This approach may leave some adult education faculty with their ideals intact, but it may also leave them unemployed.

A second approach for some adult education faculty in higher education might be to isolate their graduate programs and department from other programs and departments in colleges of education. Within this model, adult education professors might ignore other college of education programs and limit their involvement with them. They might even seek alliances across campus within other colleges, such as with training and development faculty in colleges of business, thereby ignoring their connections to colleges of education. It can be argued that this and the purist perspectives allow greater adherence to the ideals of adult education faculty but may ultimately result in the absence of adult education graduate programs in colleges of education.

A third perspective is compromise. Finding a niche for adult education programs in colleges of education involves confronting the tensions we have noted and determining where compromises may be made. From our experiences as adult educators in a college of education, professors of all age groups and disciplines have more to gain from an appreciation of their similarities than from dwelling on their differences.

At first glance, many adult education programs may not fit the K–12 paradigm of teacher preparation. It is quite a challenge to find a niche consistent with adult education values that contributes meaningfully to the mission of a college of education. An examination of the basic strengths and interests of adult education faculty may be a fruitful first step in the process. Many adult education professors have backgrounds in teaching, though their teaching backgrounds may not be in K–12 settings. Such previous teaching experience and dedication to learning in non–K–12 settings may actually be viewed as an advantage since it may provide fresh perspectives to an undergraduate teacher education program.

The adult education program at the University of Wyoming provides one example of compromise. In the early 1990s, the university's college of education developed and implemented a new teacher education program emphasizing experiential learning. As adult education faculty, we served on planning committees and developed curriculum for the new program. Our voices ensured that the concept of lifelong learning was part of the program's foundation. In addition, adult education faculty committed to teaching at least two sections of the introductory course in the undergraduate program every semester, resulting in four courses being taught by adult education faculty each year. The college would have been understaffed in the teacher education program without support from adult education faculty. Part of the new undergraduate teaching program included continuing education for teachers around the state, and adult education faculty participated in offering workshops and continuing-education classes for teachers both on and off campus. Finally, testimony from K–12 faculty colleagues supported the value of an adult education voice in the teacher education program.

The adult education faculty's participation in the undergraduate program helped secure a valued place within the college, and without having a negative impact on the department's graduate programs. The department continued to offer master's and doctoral programs on campus and through a variety of distance delivery technologies.

Although some struggle and tension continue, adult education faculty in the college of education at the University of Wyoming now have some level of security and voice in college-wide discussions pertaining to knowledge, schooling, learning, teaching, and resource allocation. For adult education programs to survive in colleges of education in higher education, compromise may be the only realistic way to address the tension resulting in differing ideals and worldviews between adult education and K–12 faculty. Principles and ideals need not be abandoned; through compromise, they may actually be strengthened when they are shared with a wider audience. Most important, adult education as a discipline may establish a more secure place to continue its work and promote its ideals if its faculty unite and fully cooperate with other college of education faculty.

References

Bloom, A. *The Closing of the American Mind.* New York: Simon & Schuster, 1987.

Dewey, J. *Democracy and Education.* Old Tappan, N.J.: Macmillan, 1916.

Ely, M. (ed.). *Handbook of Adult Education in the United States.* New York: Institute of Adult Education, Teachers College, Columbia University, 1948.

Freire, P. *Pedagogy of the Oppressed.* New York: Seabury Press, 1970.

Hart, M. *Working and Educating for Life: Feminist and International Perspectives on Adult Education.* New York: Routledge, 1992.

Hill, R. J. "Learning to Transgress: A Sociohistorical Conspectus of the American Gay Lifeworld as a Site of Struggle and Resistance." *Studies in the Education of Adults,* 1995, 28, 253–279.

Hirsch, E. D. *Cultural Literacy: What Every American Needs to Know.* New York: Vintage Books, 1988.

Illich, I. *Deschooling Society.* New York: Harper & Row, 1970.

Jensen, G., Liveright, A., and Hallenbeck, W. (eds.). *Adult Education: Outlines of an Emerging Field of University Study.* Chicago: Adult Education Association of the U.S.A., 1964.

Knowles, M. S. (ed.). *Handbook of Adult Education in the United States.* Chicago: Adult Education Association of the U.S.A., 1960.

Knowles, M. S. *The Modern Practice of Adult Education: Andragogy Versus Pedagogy.* New York: Association Press, 1970.

Knowles, M. S. *The Modern Practice of Adult Education: From Pedagogy to Andragogy.* River Grove, Ill.: Follett, 1980.

Merriam, S., and Cunningham, P. *Handbook of Adult and Continuing Education.* San Francisco: Jossey-Bass, 1990.

Office of Research and Education in Adult and Continuing Education. *RE/ACE Journal Index for Adult and Continuing Education Research.* DeKalb: Northern Illinois University, 1991.

Peters, J., and others. *Adult Education: Evolution and Achievements in a Developing Field of Study.* San Francisco: Jossey-Bass, 1991.

Rowden, D. (ed.). *Handbook of Adult Education in the United States.* New York: American Association for Adult Education, 1934.

Rowden, D. (ed.) *Handbook of Adult Education in the United States.* New York: American Association for Adult Education, 1936.

Smith, R., Aker, G., and Kidd, J. (eds.). *Handbook of Adult Education.* Old Tappan, N.J.: Macmillan, 1970.

MICHAEL J. DAY is chair and professor in the Department of Adult Learning and Technology at the University of Wyoming.

DONNA D. AMSTUTZ is associate professor in the Department of Adult Learning and Technology at the University of Wyoming.

DONNA L. WHITSON is associate professor in the Department of Adult Learning and Technology at the University of Wyoming.

5
*This chapter uses a feminist analysis to unpack how gender
and gender arrangements are constructed and maintained
through the Adult Education and Family Literacy Act.*

The Gendered Construction of the Adult Education and Family Literacy Act

Barbara Sparks

The education of adults is affected directly or indirectly by public policy written from a number of diverse sectors, including health care reform, environmental protection, labor, immigration law, social services, and K–12 education. During the recent past, we have seen ever-tightening links among education, training, and the economy. With welfare reform, we are witnessing the academic tracking of the poor into low-wage job training. The so-called concern over the achievement gap between different-colored and -classed children is refocusing attention on parental involvement in the schools for a stronger future economy. Globalization and subsequent environmental risks have spawned new social movements as educated adults react to capitalist growth.

How adults are educated, which adults are affected, and why they are educated is driven by policy concerned with preserving the economic status and well-being of the United States. The social dynamics that organize and disorganize this society are dominated by values of the market; all aspects of life have been brought under its umbrella. The Adult Education and Family Literacy Act, Title II of the Workforce Investment Act (Public Law 105–220), is no exception. In fact, the changes that occurred under the reauthorization of the Adult Education Act exemplify the strength of the new federalism that intends to control existing and changing social organizations of workers and family, men and women.

Governing relations into the local political, economic, and cultural arenas of everyday life are structured and maintained as the increased interest in state's rights and less government intrusion, or the new federalism, has secured its foothold in policy and funding, This restructuring is occurring through consolidation of programs by collapsing fifty different educational-type programs into the Workforce Investment Act, through the devolution of decision making and authority to the states by structuring three block grants to administer educational programs for literacy and employment; (National Institute for Literacy, 2000), and by accountability regimes that thinly veil economic interests. As a result, adult basic education (ABE) has been consolidated directly into employment training, progress toward employment and self-sufficiency has been made a top priority for ABE, and we have the first discretionary program to support family literacy (Public Law 105–220) with purposes of assisting adults to become literate for employment and self-sufficiency, assisting adults in completing a secondary school education, and assisting parents in gaining educational skills to become full partners in the educational development of their children. It is curious to me that the term *family literacy* made it into the name of the title, yet it represents only one of the multiple purposes of this legislation. Is this inclusion of family literacy, dressed in the guise of educational opportunity, an insertion of the conservative rhetoric of economic democracy into yet one more policy venue?

Under the rhetoric of economic democracy, human lives count less than efficiency and profits (Apple, 1996), and accountability is largely controlled and monitored by men. Daily activities are organized through "administrative procedures codified in texts and bureaucratic forms and procedures" (Naples, 1999, p. 50). As daily life is organized through policy, gender, race, and class are constructed in ways that spotlight the conservative backlash against many of the social, economic, and political gains made by women, the poor, and people of color since the 1980s.

In this chapter, I use feminist research methodology to analyze Title II to uncover its gendered nature and to explore how issues of power, interests, and difference are constructed and maintained through bureaucratic texts.

Process of Inquiry

Feminist research methodology is centered on gender and, as some feminists argue, is necessarily partial and not disinterested. It is a lens that brings into focus particular questions about power, difference, and inequalities that shape the very concrete worlds (Smith, 1987) of women's lives. It seeks to correct the invisible and the distorted.

In adult education policy analysis, feminist research speaks from a marginalized position (Skeggs, 1994; Sheared, 1998) and declares itself as situated knowledge (Haraway, 1988). Situated at the margins, feminist epistemology is concerned about the distribution of knowledge and how a particular masculinist and raced perspective becomes institutionalized through social policy, bureaucratic structures, practices, and procedures. A feminist epistemology is also concerned with what can be known, who can be a knower, and how beliefs become legitimized. Some feminists critiquing contemporary and historical male-dominated policy processes are setting the agenda for a discursive analysis that unpacks how emergent policy issues are framed (Skeggs, 1994), the dynamics of policy conflict (Sheared, 1998; Sparks, 1999), and who frames and controls the definitions emergent from the ambiguous nature of policy making (Weiss, 1995).

My feminist analysis of Title II makes problematic how the state defines and controls poor women and women of color—the majority of persons—who have been denied equal educational opportunities. Similar to a "meso analysis" that Olesen (1994) described, where there is an analysis of how social and institutional forces mesh with human activity, I am interested here in the macro, or larger, sociologic structures that reveal the effects of Title II on women in terms of gender construction and maintenance.

Ruling Relations

Taking on the problematic of the everyday world and how power works, sociologist Smith (1987, 1990) has developed a concept that can be useful to a feminist analysis of adult education. Interested in how the objectified social consciousness of men and women has come to be constructed, Smith's work has focused on an exploration of standpoint to explicate relations of ruling. She, among others, has helped us see that we have come to know the world from the standpoint of white men, to view society and social relations in terms of the interests, relevancies, and perspectives of men who are active in the relations of ruling. Capitalism created an external reality and became the exclusive terrain of men with its "extralocal, impersonal, and universalized forms of actions" (Smith, 1987, p. 5). This extralocal sphere extends beyond the "local sphere of action," where women became confined to "particularistic relationships" in the home, thus differentiating "public and private" spaces, which we have come to take for granted. The "domestic became a discrete and lesser space confining and confined to women" (Smith, 1987, p. 5).

Smith's ideas of relations of ruling are particularly helpful. She defines *relations of ruling* as "the intersection of the institutions organizing and regulating society" and as a "complex of organizing practices, including government, law, business, and financial management, professional organization, and educational institutions as well as the discourses of texts that interpenetrate the multiple sites of power" (Smith, 1987, p. 2). She goes on to say that this "mode of ruling," which dominates our society, "involves a continual transcription of the local and particular actualities of our lives in abstracted and generalized forms" (Smith, 1987, p. 2).

That policy is a text that uses "abstracted and generalized forms" can be seen by the use of terms such as *family, parent, worker, literate,* and *full partners,* prominent terms used in Title II. Women's (and other marginalized groups') experiences, realities, and voices outside the market-driven economy have been excluded; or, according to Apple (1996), "It ain't all local" (p. 109). There is only an illusion of individual, local, and particular control. Naples (1999), explicating Smith's concept of relations of ruling, states that this "continual transcription" of everyday activities is organized through codified texts and bureaucratic forms, such as educational policy, procedures, and curriculum: "These regulatory practices are derived far from the actual experiences of those whose lives these texts are designed to control" (p. 50). For example, regulating practices such as parenting classes, now included as part of the concept of family literacy, use curriculum saturated with conservative "family values" and a moral code of what constitutes a "good parent."

Because women are excluded from the power base of policy and public life, a feminist reading of Title II is necessary. At least three points can be made.

The Private Becomes Public. Smith (1987) characterizes the "local sphere of action" as the domestic realm of life assigned to women: "The functions of knowledge, judgment, and will are transferred progressively from individuals to the governing processes" (p. 5) of capitalist enterprise, bureaucratic administration, textually mediated discourse, and market processes. Public, or extralocal, discourses absorb the organizing functions originally embedded in local relationships, and domestic, everyday lived experiences are rendered invisible. Hart (1992) differentiates the private domestic sphere of women from the private haven of men, stating that the private haven connotes privacy from the government and the law, whereas the domestic sphere is a controlling patriarchal place of sexual difference. It is this domestic space that the concept of family literacy seeks to control.

With the passage of Title II, oversight of literacy practices in the home is regulated by such strategies as teaching parents "interactive literacy activities" they can use with their children; these are designated as "age-appropriate for success in school and life experience." Both methods and content are outlined in the law for the teaching and learning of literacy skills. They include phonemic awareness, systematic phonics, fluency, and reading comprehension based on the work of the National Institute of Child Health and Human Development (Public Law 105–220, sec. 242).

According to testimony of Andrew Hartman, director of the National Institute for Literacy, at a subcommittee hearing on the reauthorization of adult education, "the literacy gap poses a serious challenge to meeting several major national goals, including parental involvement in schools" (U.S. Senate, 1995, pp. 16–17). Family literacy, he says, is essential to building strong families and communities. Society's problems have become problems with families. Thus, intrusion into the private space of family life and parenting, legitimized by legislative hearings and reports, is justified as essential in meeting U.S. national goals. Under Title II, parents are to become "the primary teacher for their children" and "full partners in the educational development of their children" (Public Law 105–220, sec. 202). In partnership with Even Start programs, which use home-based services to engage more parents from families designated as being at risk, defined as those living in poverty, those who lack English proficiency, and those headed by teen parents, ABE is now prioritized to promote "family values" under the guise of parents as "full partners" in the education of their children.

"Parent" as Mother. In reference to this analysis, it is helpful to know that according to Laubach Literacy Action's "Facts About Women's Lives," 23 percent (cited in Imel, 1996) of the women in the United States over the age of twenty-five have not gone beyond high school or the general educational development. Carmack's historical perspective (1992) of women's unequal access to education points to the societal mandates regulating women's lives as well as the religious beliefs that have served to reinforce the traditional role and status of women.

Considering the gender divisions within the dominant traditional family, family literacy and parental involvement in children's literacy is a gender issue hidden within the rhetoric. Mothers are the targets of the emphasis in Title II on family literacy, whether they live in traditional families or not. Low-skilled women on welfare, mandated into ABE, vocational training, and then work, are single mothers who must become economically self-sufficient. They are equally hidden within the rhetoric of family literacy. As family literacy becomes increasingly public and legitimized through government policy, mothers in the United States, similarly to mothers in Great Britain (David, 1991), are now expected to take on the responsibility of education, as well as mothering and paid employment.

According to Moore and Stavrianos (1995), 61 percent of new enrollments in federal ABE programs are women. Furthermore, 45 percent of all new ABE clients between the ages of sixteen and fifty-five are nonwhite, with Latino-origin individuals making up the largest proportion. The population of those enrolled in ABE, as indicated by these figures, is predominantly women and, as we can infer from the numbers, women of color. In a study of adult literacy programs in several states since the passage of Title II, H. Beder (personal communication, Nov. 17, 2000) has found that all participants enrolled in parenting programs associated with family literacy are women, an indication of the hegemonic and legitimating power of public policy.

Analyzing the K–12 education reform movement, Weiss (1995) argues for the inclusion of gender equality, stating that since *A Nation at Risk* (National Commission on Excellence in Education, 1983) was made public, various educational commissions, task forces, and reports have totally ignored gender inequality. She insists that the education reform movement must take seriously gender inequalities. We can extend this to adult education and family literacy reform. Research, program reports and evaluations, and adult literacy practice have documented the gender inequalities of ABE, yet legislators ignore what is publicly known.

Purposes of Literacy for Women. According to Greg Hart, director of Pima County (Arizona) Adult Education, "The link between a child's potential for educational success and the educational level of his/her parents, in particular the mother, is indisputable. Adult Education programs working with parents, especially in *family literacy partnerships* with schools and early childhood education providers are *helping to positively transform the futures of families and communities throughout the country*" (U.S. Senate, 1995, p. 59).

In family literacy programs initiated under Even Start, the focus is on the child's literacy development, and the mother is educated in order to teach her children. The mother thus serves a role in the child's development. In traditional ABE programs, women's literacy has a broader focus, which addresses both her multiple roles and her personal desires; in other words, literacy is valued in its own right for multiple tasks but is not limited to the exclusive role of primary teacher. The rhetoric we find in Title II is that of childhood literacy, now privileged over that of adult literacy. The ramifications are tremendous. Curriculum is focused on the child, with the needs and interests of the child taking center stage. Adult literacy teaching strategies move into training the mother how to teach her children and embed conservative family values within nostalgically idealized motherhood (Skeggs, 1994). Part of being a "good mother" means teaching and partnering with educational experts. During the early 1980s, we saw the political struggle for funding between early childhood education and adult literacy. As early childhood programs gained support in Colorado, where I worked in the adult literacy field, we saw resistance to adult literacy–focused programs, whereas programs targeted to children were promoted under the rhetoric that "children are our future."

That increasing educational opportunities for women are needed is not in doubt. What is in question is that the intent, or the purpose, of that education is being mandated to focus on family literacy at the expense of personal goals and a wider interpretation of adult literacy needs. Women's needs have been subordinated to the needs of the family and the patriarchal system. While women often relate an interest in learning to read so they can read to their children, they typically have more personal goals, which they may be hesitant to articulate because of the social pressures against ambitions that may be viewed as selfish (Cuban and Hayes, 1996). Yet according to Hart (1996), critical literacy is essential to the work of mothering and the work of supporting and sustaining life itself.

Policy Research Implications

Feminist analysis of educational public policy exposes how power, difference, and inequality work through relations of ruling. As Weiss (1995) states, "We cannot afford to take the position that schools [or adult education policy or programs] simply mirror society and that they, therefore, have no responsibility to address the conditions under which certain forms of gender construction and relations are shaped" (p. 188). The regressive and conservative backlash has become strong enough to ignore policy research about the inequalities in ABE. Nevertheless, continued attempts to influence the development of policy are needed similar to that which is occurring through various research efforts connected with the 2002 reauthorization of welfare reform where such gendered issues as women's education, child care, health care, a living wage, and coercive implementation strategies are being addressed.

Adult education policy should be reexamined because of the contradictions and competing interests between women's development for parenting (through family literacy) and women's development for work (through welfare reform). It is also clear that the feminization of the literacy practitioner workforce, including volunteers as well as students, is an important issue. We need to critique the differences between men's literacy development for the workforce and women's literacy development for the home and the competition between men and women for limited spaces within ABE programs. This issue is voiced by Senator Jim Jeffords: "Most of the welfare recipients are women, which will mean that you will be shutting out opportunities for male adults" (U.S. Senate, 1995, p. 88). Furthermore, we need gendered analyses of how lives of class and race are differentially constructed and maintained among groups of women. Finally, there is a need to conduct feminist analysis of the links between educational policy and program implementation.

Resources

Apple, M. *Cultural Politics and Education.* New York: Teachers College Press. 1996.

Carmack, N. "Women and Illiteracy: The Need for Gender Specific Programming in Literacy Education." *Adult Basic Education,* 1992, *2,* 176–194.

Cuban, S., and Hayes, E. "Women in Family Literacy Programs: A Gendered Perspective." In P. A. Sissel (ed.), *Community-Based Approach to Literacy Programs.* New Directions for Adult and Continuing Education, no. 70. San Francisco: Jossey-Bass, 1996.

David, S. "A Gender Agenda: Women and the Family in the New ERA?" *British Journal of Sociology of Education,* 1991, *12,* 433–446.

Haraway, D. "Situated Knowledges: The Science Question in Feminism and the Privilege of Partial Perspective." *Feminist Studies,* 1988, *14,* 575–599.

Hart, M. *Working and Educating for Life: Feminist and International Perspectives on Adult Education.* New York: Routledge, 1992.

Hart, M., with Russell, A., and De Arrudah, E. "Literacy and Motherwork." In UNESCO Institute for Education, *Alpha 96 Basic Education and Work.* Toronto: Culture Concepts Publishers, 1996.

Imel, S. "Women and Literacy." In *ERIC Trends and Issues.* Washington, D.C.: ERIC Clearinghouse on Adult, Career, and Vocational Education, 1996.

Moore, M., and Stavrianos, M. *Review of Adult Education Programs and Their Effectiveness: A Background Paper for Reauthorization of the Adult Education Act.* Washington, D.C.: U.S. Department of Education, 1995.

Naples, N. "Towards Comparative Analyses of Women's Political Praxis: Explicating Multiple Dimensions of Standpoint Epistemology for Feminist Ethnography." *Women and Politics*, 1999, *20*, 29–56.

National Commission on Excellence in Education. *A Nation at Risk: The Imperative for Educational Reform*. Washington, D.C.: U.S. Department of Education, 1983.

National Institute for Literacy. "Policy Update: Workforce Investment Act Offers Opportunities for Adult and Family Literacy." [www.nifl.gov/policy/98-9-23.htm]. Oct. 18, 2000.

Olesen, V. "Feminisms and Models of Qualitative Research." In N. Denzin and Y. Lincoln (eds.), *Handbook of Qualitative Research*. Thousand Oaks, Calif.: Sage, 1994.

Sheared, V. *Race, Gender, and Welfare Reform: The Elusive Quest for Self-Determination*. New York: Garland, 1998.

Skeggs, B. "The Constraints of Neutrality: The 1988 Education Reform Act and Feminist Research." In D. Halpin and B. Troyna (eds.), *Researching Education Policy: Ethical and Methodological Issues*. Bristol, Pa.: Falmer Press, 1994.

Smith, D. *The Everyday as Problematic: A Feminist Sociology*. Boston: Northeastern University Press, 1987.

Smith, D. *The Conceptual Practices of Power: A Feminist Sociology of Knowledge*. Boston: Northeastern University Press, 1990.

Sparks, B. "Critical Issues and Dilemmas for Adult Literacy Programs Under Welfare Reform." In L. Martin and J. Fisher (eds.), *The Welfare-to-Work Challenge for Adult Literacy Workers*. New Directions for Adult and Continuing Education, no. 83. San Francisco: Jossey-Bass, 1999.

U.S. Senate. Committee on Labor and Human Resources. "Adult Education and Family Literacy Reform Act." Hearing before the Subcommittee on Education, Arts, and Humanities, 104th Cong., 1st sess., May 19, 1995.

Weiss, L. "Gender and the Reports: The Missing Piece." In R. Ginsberg and D. Plank (eds.), *Commissions, Reports, Reforms, and Educational Policy*. New York: Praeger, 1995.

BARBARA SPARKS is assistant professor in the Department of Adult and Community College Education, North Carolina State University, Raleigh.

6

Adult literacy and basic education are governed by political processes that are similar to feudalism. New trends point the way to a democratizing of knowledge in literacy.

Living in the Feudalism of Adult Basic and Literacy Education: Can We Negotiate a Literacy Democracy?

B. Allan Quigley

Imagine that you are a farmer in the era of feudalism. Like all of the other farmers in your region, you survive on the largesse of your landowner. He takes your annual harvest and provides for most of your basic needs in return. You and your family are totally dependent on him for your survival. Knowing only this version of reality, you take it as normal.

To confuse normality, however, the landowner, ostensibly in consultation with the king, frequently changes his mind about the type of crops that should be planted. You know that wheat grows best on one field and oats on another, but in some years, the landowner dictates that this year's crop needs to be beans. Another year, flax is decreed or hay. Some can even remember when all farmers were told to raise pigs.

There are various village committees where you can discuss selected issues and cautiously make suggestions, but you know you really have no serious input. After all, you are only a farmer, and this is the feudal era. You have no clout.

You finally seek to negotiate the political landscape by learning to listen carefully to the rumor mill within the farm community. This is mainly why you sit on the village committees. You also begin to find other ways to keep the farm viable by planting some grain that you know will give a high yield (of course, you do not mention these activities to the landlord).

Probably the most frightening and divisive part of your existence in this reality is that you need to submit a plan for the future of your farm every spring. In fact, every farmer is encouraged to bid on each other's farm. This

New Directions for Adult and Continuing Education, no. 91, Fall 2001   © John Wiley & Sons, Inc.

means that if someone puts in a more favorable proposal on how to run your farm, you and your family will have to leave. It is not even always clear that the favored plan is based on the announced criteria. Politics always prevail.

In order to survive, you use some devious negotiation skills. You and other farmers have noticed that the landowner only asks for *reports* of what you are growing. And when the landlord's men visit, they barely know what they are looking at—to them, beans look like oats and oats look like wheat—so sometimes your annual harvest report says you grew beans when you actually grew wheat.

You have noticed that good farmers are leaving when they get the chance.

But this is not the feudal era; this is literacy education in the twenty-first century, a time when the resources in the Western world are at an all-time high but nearly 50 percent of adults in the United States (Kirsch, Jungeblut, Jenkins, and Kolstad, 1993) and almost 40 percent of the adults in Canada (Statistics Canada, 1996) still face difficulty with literacy. Despite cries for the eradication of illiteracy across the continent through most of the past century, support for adult basic education and literacy (ABLE) is about as unpredictable as feudal crop policies: your ABLE program survives year by year with bids on annual grants, you live off the rumor mill, everyone you know in ABLE seeks the favors of the state or provincial director, and everyone speculates on what is in the mind of the federal director of adult education and his or her political masters.

In truth, situational ethics is occasionally used in your program for the sake of survival. Your program administrator has tried to find other sources of income, such as trying to convince members of the corporate sector to help sponsor your program and fundraising campaigns. Humiliating as it may be, your program probably now has a charity number. Despite the fact that federal funds (calculated in 1997 constant dollars) fell from $309 per enrollee in 1970, to $95 in 1980, and to just $66 per student in 1990 (National Institute for Literacy, 2000), few in the public domain know that funding is woefully inadequate compared with any other educational system. Similarly, despite the expectations of the state, teachers typically teach what the students need and want, and insinuate (and report on) the current ABLE policy thrust when necessary. They raise wheat and report beans. It all takes its toll on practice.

After centuries of democracy in North America, we live in an inherited feudalistic system of direct and indirect controls over the politics and pedagogy of ABLE. In this chapter, I discuss what this means to most teachers and tutors (here both referred to as teachers) and administrators. Although I touch on some suggestions for survival negotiations, my primary purpose is to discuss how a new type of negotiation might be used to move the political landscape of ABLE toward a democracy of knowledge and practice.

After some thirty years in and around literacy education, including work in government, I have no illusions on how difficult a widespread move toward democratizing literacy will be. However, I also know that it is deceptively easy to be complacent or cynical in this field. We need many, many things in ABLE, and above all else, we need hope for the future.

New Winds, Sweeping Changes, and the Power of the Past

Empowering new ways of communicating and exciting new ways of creating and sharing knowledge are arising across the fields of literacy. Finding a collective voice and the creation and ownership of new knowledge are key elements in building a professional field of practice. If democratization and change are to occur in the future, we will need to enhance these important directions. However, I also believe the field needs to know its own stories better. In this sense, we need to improve and document our collective memory in order to see where we have been, what has been tried, and who our heroes are.

The legacy of losing memory in ABLE is a serious issue. The endless staff turnover in ABLE and the perpetual rediscovery of the program wheel through the spinning of legislative thrusts all conspire to help us forget where we have traveled. Indeed, the hegemony of literacy politics encourages us to pretend there is no past in literacy education. As Smith (1977) once put it, "Over the years, in times of crisis, the main body of Americans kept rediscovering the literacy problems and, over the years, hastily contrived solutions to the problem were invented or reinvented. As the crisis passed, so did the concern of America's leaders" (p. vi). However, with loss of memory comes a vulnerability to believing that the latest hastily contrived solution is the best solution. For instance, without some background, it is easy to assume that ABLE comes at bargain basement prices. In 1993, for instance, the U.S. expenditure per elementary and secondary student per academic year was $6,285. It cost only $235 for each ABLE student in the same year (Beder, 1994). It is also easy to assume that ours is naturally a field comprising volunteers and part-time practitioners, but this was certainly not always the case. Today, "few full time jobs are available for adult education and literacy instructors, and those that are available offer low pay and few (if any) benefits" (National Institute for Literacy, 2000, p. 20).

Losing memory leads us to assume that today's inherited ABLE system is somehow normal. In fact, we have learned to survive in a state of political expediency by often doing the right things for the wrong reasons (Cook, 1977; Quigley, 1997).

We can imagine a better world for literacy. If we can create and own our own knowledge, communicate as practitioners and students of literacy across our vast geography, and be more cognizant of the stories of our past, I believe we can build a better world for our learners and our field. However, let us first problematize the world we know for a minute by glimpsing it through the lens of the feudal metaphor being used here.

Negotiating in the World We Know

To see the feudal system at work in ABLE, one simply needs to pick up a conference program at almost any of the annual state or most of the provincial conferences of adult education. There will typically be found an innocuous-looking session entitled, "An Update on the New [fill in the blank with the most recent state or federal policy initiative]." Like the farmer attending to the rumor mill, this session is vital for administrators. This is a platform for the state director to update the field by informing them of what they can expect in the coming year. This session is about keeping the farm and knowing what to plant next spring.

At a recent statewide adult education ABLE conference I attended, the state director skillfully explained the upcoming Workforce Investment Act (WIA) and gave details on what was later to become the National Reporting System (NRS) for the field: a set of criteria for measuring and reporting student learning outcomes (with repercussions if programs did not succeed in these measures).

At the risk of oversimplifying, the director explained that the impending WIA would seek to move ABLE students into the workforce as directly as possible. As the very title of the legislation suggests, ABLE teachers and administrators would (again) be seen as part of an investment in the labor force. What was definitely new was that the workforce goals would be assessed and duly reported through the NRS, the first ever.

The state director's lengthy update brought the room to a state of complete silence. Then the questions began: "How does this differ from the earlier workforce legislation back in the 1970s, like the Job Training Partnership Act?" "Who will administer the questions necessary to complete the NRS when there are not enough staff to do what is now required?" Despite assurances that "nothing was set in stone," in fact the answers given said: "Thank you for your questions, but we are looking at some very major events and are talking about a very big picture here."

Having once served as the equivalent of a state director, I know this is an extremely difficult session for most state directors. While educators are assumed to be engaged in the pursuit of informed dissent, civil servants are expected to engage in the pursuit of controlled consent (Quigley, 1997). It is this "beyond-our-reach" notion in the politics of negotiating ABLE that I would hope administrators, teachers, and researchers could ultimately change. And it is changing.

New Ways for Negotiating the Future

According to many recent academics and writers, we are well past a time when all things modern are believed to be best. We are now in a postmodern era, when previously held beliefs, institutions, and political ideologies are in doubt. Bigger is not necessarily better; scientists are often wrong; the latest breakthrough has often done more harm than good. Yet despite growing doubts across Western culture, authors such as Aronowitz and Giroux (1991) also argue that the stage is set for entirely new voices to be heard: "Read in more positive terms, postmodernists are arguing for a plurality of voices and narratives—that is, for different narratives that present the unpresentable" (p. 69). It is my argument that the prevailing feudal order in ABLE is under increasing pressure from within. The growing expression of doubt in what is taken to be the accepted norm in ABLE, together with more articulated doubts concerning both the motives and the wisdom of those who "can't know what's best," is a growing counterhegemony that cannot be ignored. The hope here is that literacy will be pushed to become more democratic through the power of combined voices and knowledge.

Using the Internet Revolution for Negotiated Change. The updates on the impending WIA and its attendant NRS throughout 1997, 1998, and 1999 brought about the widest, and possibly the most forceful, discussion that ABLE has ever seen around new legislation. Several Internet Web sites carried information on the new legislation, but the listserv moderated by David Rosen, executive director of the Adult Literacy Resource Institute in Boston, on behalf of the National Institute for Literacy, carried 1,196 messages in 1999. A scan of the messages indicates that well over 80 percent of them were on the WIA and NRS debate or closely related issues. Many were posed directly to the Office of Vocational and Adult Education at the U.S. Office of Education. In December 1999, the director of that office, Ron Pugsley, posted eighteen replies to practitioner questions.

One group of participants on the listserv argued for a moratorium on this legislation. Others argued vehemently against the implementation of the NRS. For instance, Tom Sticht, director of Applied Behavioral and Cognitive Sciences, posed a series of research-based criticisms on the mandatory requirements of the NRS. Katherine King at Fordham University asked, "Doesn't this powerfully insistent, blind manditoriness, and utterly unbending power [of the NRS requirements] serve to dull our creative understanding of ourselves by taking away a public trust invested in us as teachers?" (2000, p. 2). Some tried to advocate alternative directions. However, Larry Fraller (2000), an ABE teacher, caught the tone of the issue by asking: "What happened to REPRESENTATIVE democracy?" adding, "Why [do] we let business minded people make our decisions for us in education? . . . Legislators and other administrators are taking it into their hands to run literacy programs, indeed ALL education programs as a business. Where'd THAT idea ever get started?" (p. 2).

But did the debate make a difference? This NIFL listserv discussion and the direct contacts made from the field to policymakers evidently became part of the National Literacy Summit in the summer of 2000. At this summit, representatives of literacy discussed the impending legislation. A follow-up report from Carolyn Staley (2000) stated that "the staff of NIFL has read through every response over the past weeks, and has been synthesizing the comments, organizing them around priorities, and looking for broad themes that may be emerging. . . . The current thinking is that some of the priorities may be able to be combined, and that the final priority areas will be fewer and slightly reorganized" (p. 1).

Far from the hopes of those who argued for a moratorium, nevertheless, the wide discussion involved in this debate far surpassed previous legislative debates. For the first time, anyone with access to a computer and a modem could raise his or her voice and be heard on policy formation.

This most recent event leaves the field with a challenge well posed by George Demetrion (2000), then manager of the Literacy Volunteers of Greater Hartford program: "Does govt [sic] need to be responsive to these voices from the field . . . or should the NLA, in all its diversity, serve as the Fourth Estate for ABE/Literacy that should be tapped into and consulted *before* and while policy is being established? Should policy formulations emerge in part *from* discussions on the NLA?" (p. 3). If Aronowitz and Giroux (1991) are right, the answer to Demetrion's question will come not from the state or the federal government but from the new, stronger, collective identity of our field. History teaches that such collective voices will not and cannot go ignored in a democratic society.

The Revolution of Practitioner-Based Research. LeCompte and de Marrais (1992) have argued that "those who control production of knowledge also control the definition of truth, and in turn, the definition of reality" (p. 15). Elsewhere, I (1997) have discussed how recurrent literacy has supported negative stereotypes of low-literate adults as reality. This has only helped marginalize our field by association. If LeCompte and de Marrais (1992) are right, there is an important grassroots movement of practice-based research arising across the field—a movement where creating and owning our own knowledge is lending itself to a practice-based definition of truth and, I hope, a democratization of literacy knowledge

Much has happened in the past two decades of literacy research. Besides a much more significant body of credible quantitative and qualitative research literature coming from university-based researchers, the past few years have also seen the rise of a new practitioner-based capacity for creating research. With a postmodern turn, this is arising from a new, critical way of seeing in practice (Quigley and Kuhne, 1997).

Across the United States, Canada, Australia, the United Kingdom, Europe, Africa, and Latin America, literacy practitioners have become increasingly involved in participatory research, collaborative research, and practitioner action research (Quigley and Kuhne, 1997). One of the most extensive publications on practitioner-based research in community settings is Hautecouer's *Alpha 94* (1994), with dozens of case studies of local projects that improved literacy and the local economy in Southern Europe, Central Europe, and North America.

The widening impact of practitioner research in North America is also being reported and discussed (Quigley and Kuhne, 1997). Practitioner-based critical reflection is leading to regular critiques within our communities of practice. Action research in both informal and institutional contexts has been shown by authors such as Brooks and Watkins (1994) to be a viable means toward democratizing the work place. This movement can help bring the field of adult literacy education toward a more credible role in the policy formation discourse. It can help counter some of the damaging stereotypes of literacy. And it can help us critique more of the "hastily contrived solutions" (Smith, 1977, p. vi) so endemic to the politics of literacy. Here is the rise of a new potential to learn from practice and to advise with authority from the grassroots.

Everything I Ever Needed to Know, I Learned from Robin Hood

Nothing really changes without shifts in the balance of power. To negotiate our field toward a democracy of literacy, I believe we should increase our engagement in the three growing activities briefly discussed here. First, research in practice has the potential to influence, if not transform, the researcher, the participants, our literacy settings, and the literacy culture we share. I believe more practitioners should learn about and engage in forms of literacy practitioner research (Quigley, 1997) and use their newly found knowledge to inform practice and policies. Second, the WIA debate had opened a new door for this field. The Internet revolution is enabling practitioners, academics, policymakers, and students to be part of an unprecedented communication revolution in ABLE. This too is a major step toward a new era of negotiation. Finally, if more practitioners and students can become better informed by the lessons of the past—the lessons of policy, research, and practice—and if more can learn about our heroes and successes, the confidence in the literally thousands of voices across this field can play a greater role in the civil society of the future. The dream of a new era of literacy democracy can become our reality.

References

Aronowitz, S., and Giroux, H. *Postmodern Education: Politics, Culture and Social Criticism.* Minneapolis: University of Minnesota Press, 1991.

Beder, H. "The Current Status of Adult Literacy Education in the United States." *PAACE Journal of Lifelong Learning,* 1994, *3,* 14–25.

Brooks, A., and Watkins, K. E. (eds.). *The Emerging Power of Action Inquiry Technologies.* New Directions for Adult and Continuing Education, no. 63. San Francisco: Jossey-Bass, 1994.

Cook, W. *Adult Literacy Education in the United States.* Newark, Del.: International Reading Association, 1977.

Demetrion, G. "NLA: NRS Discussion." In Literacy NLA Forum. [www.nifl.gov/hifl-nla.] June 12, 2000.

Fraller, L. "WLA Discussion: Summit; Business, a Teacher's Perspective." In NLA Discussion: Summit. [www.nifl.gov/lincs/discussion/nifl-nla.html]. Jan. 19, 2000.

Hautecouer, J. (ed.). *Alpha 94: Literacy and Cultural Development Strategies in Rural Areas.* Toronto: Culture Concepts, 1994.

King, K. "WLA Discussion: Summit; Business, a Teacher's Perspective." In NLA Discussion: Summit. [www.nifl.gov/lincs/discussion/nifl-nla.html]. Jan. 19, 2000.

Kirsch, I., Jungeblut, A., Jenkins, L., and Kolstad, A. *Adult Literacy in America.* Washington, D.C.: Department of Education, 1993.

LeCompte, M., and de Marrais, E. "The Disempowering of Empowerment: Out of Revolution and into the Classroom." *Educational Foundations,* 1992, *6,* 5–32.

National Institute for Literacy. *Literacy Skills for 21st Century America: A Blueprint for Creating a More Literate Nation.* Washington, D.C.: National Institute for Literacy, 2000.

Quigley, A. *Rethinking Literacy Education: The Critical Need for Practice-Based Change.* San Francisco: Jossey-Bass, 1997.

Quigley, A., and Kuhne, G. (eds.). *Creating Practical Knowledge.* New Directions for Adult and Continuing Education, no. 73. San Francisco: Jossey-Bass, 1997.

Smith, E. A. "Foreword." In W. Cook, *Adult Literacy Education in the United States.* Newark, Del.: International Reading Association, 1977.

Staley, C. "NLA Info: Summit Update." In NLA Info: Summit Update. [www.nifl.gov/lincs/discussion/nifl-nla.html]. July 21, 2000.

Statistics Canada. *International Adult Literacy Survey. Reading the Future: A Portrait of Literacy in Canada.* Ottawa, Ont.: Ministry of Industry, 1996.

Sticht, T. "NLA Discussion: WIA/NRS." Literacy NLA Forum. [www.nifl.gov/nifl-nla.]

B. ALLAN QUIGLEY *is associate professor of adult education at St. Francis Xavier University, Antigonish, Nova Scotia.*

7

This chapter explores the political hot spots within the American Association for Adult and Continuing Education that provide a backdrop for its focus, or lack thereof, on educational public policy.

Political Hotbeds: Professional Organizations as Policymakers

Phyllis M. Cunningham

Professional organizations should be a place for collective action directed toward policies for the public good and a place for debating issues among members. They often fall short on both counts (American Association for Adult and Continuing Education, 1999). This chapter looks at the recent record on these goals by the American Association of Adult Continuing Education (AAACE) and its two largest subgroups: the Commission of Professors of Adult Education (CPAE) and the Commission of Adult Basic Education (COABE). In doing so, I compare them with the activities of the structurally separate but closely allied Adult Education Research Conference (AERC).

I assess the participatory nature of the AAACE, the dominant ideology as expressed by the leadership and in its conference programming, and how knowledge about issues was or was not cultivated. I also compare the politics of the AERC, the research arm of the CPAE, with that of the AAACE, as well as take note of the emergence of two new organizations, the Academy of Human Resource Development (AHRD) and the North American Alliance of Popular Adult Educators (NAAPAE). This appraisal is derived from my perspective as a member since 1969 of what is now the AAACE, from having attended the CPAE and the AERC for thirty years, and as one of the leaders who founded the NAAPAE in 1994. I see myself as a critical social theorist; I champion free, open participation within groups. For me, one of the central goals of adult education is building civil society. My bias is that normative decisions should be made by maximizing participation in the process.

New Directions for Adult and Continuing Education, no. 91, Fall 2001 © John Wiley & Sons, Inc.

The Politics of Social Justice

The 1977 Adult Education Association (AEA) conference in Detroit stands out in my mind. The social justice activists, led by John Ohliger and Tom Heaney, two activist-scholars in adult education, held a rump conference to raise concerns on the extremes of professionalism. In the year that followed, this group met at Highlander Research and Education Center in New Market, Tennessee, long known for radical adult education, to develop an agenda. At that meeting, the National Alliance of Voluntary Learning (NAVL) was formed to challenge mandatory continuing education (MCE) and to stress the importance of nonformal adult education. At the 1979 AEA Boston conference, the politics of market-led adult education was challenged around the issue of MCE, an issue selected by the Highlander group. Buttons were distributed, and a newsletter, *NAVL Gazing,* was issued daily from the borrowed office of John Holt, the prominent deschooler. Two resolutions on the issue of MCE were presented for debate at the delegate assembly, and the air was electric as members talked about the issues. President Violet Malone established an MCE task force to present a written report to help the association guide policy development at the next conference (AEA-USA Task Force). This was the last conference when general open debate on issues occurred.

At the Salt Lake City conference in 1990, the program organizers (Phyllis Safman, Gary Eyre, and Lorraine Zinn) tried to raise the fundamental question of mission through a debate in a general session. During the debate, AAACE was charged, and found guilty, by the program organizers of dereliction in failing to honor its founding commitment to educate adults to participate in democratic social action. At this 1990 conference, the president, W. S. Griffith, set up a social action committee, and in November 1991, one of its members, Jack Mezirow, presented a five-page policy paper, "Faded Visions and Fresh Commitments: Adult Education's Social Goals." But the issue of social justice was dead on arrival, for there was no structure within the association to support continued dialogue. According to one member of the committee, "Jack Mezirow found that his paper was literally buried by the staff of AAACE in Washington—as it was too radical." Except for *Adult Learning,* a journal that provided a venue for some discussion of the issues, no other place within the association allowed for democratic exchange. Rather, the face-to-face structure of the delegate assembly, an entity that historically had had a measure of power in the decision-making apparatus of AAACE, was eliminated, along with the Social Philosophy Luncheon, a forum for social activists dating back to Eduard Lindeman (Mezirow, 1991).

Were these changes maliciously devised to prevent participation of the membership? I do not think so. I think that the juggernaut of "learning for earning" was overtaking the association with little challenge from the leadership. The efficiency and effectiveness of scientific rationality and the uncritical acceptance of human capital theory became the invisible force within the organization.

The Merger

To understand the AAACE and the withdrawal in 1999 of its largest commission, COABE, is to recognize that this relationship has historically been tenuous. The first American Association of Adult Education (AAAE) was founded in 1926 with the help of the Carnegie Foundation. At that time, there was also a growing group of adult educators in the Department of Immigration in the National Education Association. The AAAE prided itself on being a broad umbrella organization, bringing groups of adult educators together regardless of where they worked. The Department of Immigration also began to broaden its membership, changing its name to the Department of Adult Education. Eventually, these two organizations joined in 1951 to form the AEA. The next year, those members working in the public school sector organized the National Association of Public School Adult Educators (NAPSAE), a group within but independent of the AEA. This organization became completely independent by 1957. In 1982, the AEA and NAPSAE again merged to become the AAACE. This merger lasted until 1999, when the COABE, whose membership is dominated by public school and community college adult basic and literacy educators, withdrew from the AAACE, taking an estimated 74 percent of the membership with it (D. Amstutz, personal communication with the author, Nov. 11, 2000).

It was in the merger of 1982 that a hierarchical structure for decision making was devised. This centralized structure then led to the increased power of the Washington permanent staff over the elected temporary leadership. A new executive director was hired in 1990, in part because he had political experience and it was thought that he would understand the Washington culture. Lobbying was seen as a high priority, so that even with a deficit budget we hired a paid lobbyist (Allbritton, 1997). In the end, we were hoisted on our own petard, as our association business was outsourced to Washington technical experts with no background in adult education, and the commissions within the association were manipulated into paying the bill. Creative Washington budgeting allowed a $100,000 debt to be reported as a balanced budget (McVey, 1997; AAACE, 1996). In fact, COABE contributed $280,000 to AAACE's debt when that commission undertook its separation from the parent organization (D. Amstutz, personal communication with the author, Nov. 11, 2000).

Given this untenable situation, why was the membership upset when COABE and CPAE issued resolutions of no confidence against the executive director during the general business meeting in 1998? An analysis of both the inner workings of the association and its ideology provides the explanation.

Membership Participation

One major role of AAACE has been to engage the country's political apparatus through its membership. This being the case, then, we must ask why
AAACE's headquarters have been in Washington, D.C., why those outside
adult education were selected to run the organization, and why power ultimately resided in the staff rather than in the democratically elected board
of directors.

I would first argue that having "beltway elites" to lobby for legislation
that affects members is clearly nonparticipatory. Don't our senators and representatives come from local legislative and senatorial districts? Isn't there
a saying that all politics is local? Can't we mobilize and educate our members on policy initiatives? Of course, we could, if we thought participation
and a critically informed membership were key to our politics. Second, we
must ask what has been the goal of our lobbying. Have we lobbied for
antiracist education, peace education, AIDS or public health education,
tribal education, community-based education, humanities education, and
environmental education? No; we have not (Cunningham, 1996). Instead,
we uncritically push adult basic education (ABE), vocational education,
workforce investment education, and other public policy initiatives that are
constructed on a deficiency discourse paradigm and have as their goal
preparation for employment. We lobby for jobs, not for effecting educational
policy. We lobby through experts; we do not bring our members as intellectuals to the table to debate issues.

This is not to say that "market demand" is not worthy of our interest.
It was concerned adult educators who developed a plan to contextualize
literacy, arguing not only for workforce but family, community, and church
contextualized literacy programs (Fingeret and Jurmo, 1989). The very
successful family literacy programs have their genesis in local efforts of
adult educators, who then developed the policy initiative to bring it into
legislation.

In summary, the membership was not engaged in educating their legislators or deciding what the goal of the policy development was to be.
Rather, the tail wagged the dog in that those who were not adult educators
became the spokespersons.

Dominant Ideology

Given this structural framework, how can the dominant ideology of the
organization be described? Rather than active participants, members were
treated as objects; they were there to pay dues and attend conferences. This
symbolic violence on its members was also perpetuated by the association's
culture when leaders financially squeezed individual members and their
subgroups. As a result, COABE could not control its own funds garnered by
its successful, well-attended national conferences and an energized mem-

bership. COABE had a democratically developed mission statement, a strategic plan, targeted goals, and a journal, and it provided member services and had over $275,000 in the bank. COABE's offers of help to AAACE were unheeded except for the money.

The CPAE, with less money in its coffers (about $9,000) but a predisposition for autonomy was pressured by the AAACE staff (CPAE, 2000). It was not allowed to exist as a preconference, the integrity of its meetings collapsed, and a quarterly issue of its research journal was canceled in order to conserve funds (Adult Education Quarterly Editorial Board, 1997). Its membership, formerly closed to professors, was opened to the entire association, which was a problem for some, but over which the CPAE had no control. In fact, the restructuring of the board by deleting the elected commission's leadership and replacing it with at-large elections essentially neutered the commission's voices (D. Amstutz, personal communication to the author, Jan. 17, 2001). Reasons for this bullying were said to be the Internal Revenue Service (IRS) rules. Some felt that the board was complicit, but with good reason: they were reminded that in the end, they were the ones who would be accountable economically to the IRS (V. Sheared, personal communication to the author, Jan. 10, 2001).

Symbolic violence could also be seen in the association's emblems, its cultural signs. At no other national adult education conference could one experience the jingoistic obsession with large U.S. flags and uniformed troops parading in lockstep—and one asks, "Why?" Five years ago in Charlotte, North Carolina, the entire conference was held outside the exhibits for over thirty minutes so that Miss America could lead everyone into the exhibit area. What does the concept of Miss America mean to conference goers? Why is Miss America parading at our conference if it is not to celebrate a socially constructed concept of women as physical beauty and coy female personality? Many members found this offensive.

And what about the substance of our conference? What was at issue here? In order to ensure maximum attendance at conferences, the jurying procedures appeared to become lax. Many submissions for workshops were accepted and scheduled, resulting in no-shows at many sessions. Yet there was no penalty attached for nondelivery. It was as if attendance was the goal, and the workshops themselves were irrelevant. Conferences are scheduled in locations that detract from what the conferences are supposed to be about—for example, Atlantic City and Disneyland. Conference goers stay at expensive hotels where the kickback to the association helps leverage money from institutions and encourage members to use "353 funds" (professional development money) from the states (Allbritton, 1997) available to support some members. But if this is considered appropriate, who comes to the meetings? Not the volunteer, not the student, not the community adult educator. So whose knowledge gets promoted in this kind of structure? The biases were well mobilized to constrict research and theory to those ideas supportive of the dominant structures.

At the 1995 Kansas City conference, the Social Philosophy Luncheon was cancelled, and in fact, it was deleted permanently. When the social activists clamored for time to have a speaker, the last of the three speakers scheduled for general sessions was asked to share the platform. The subject matter of the general sessions at this conference was instructive. At the first session, a human resource development trainer regaled everyone with the imperative of "adding value" or being laid off. She told us how her company's personnel were always "plugged in" at the office and in the field by cell phone, fax, and computer, and to be unavailable was to risk discharge. She was sharp, commanding, and a virtual lexicon for market power. Opposite her was a local community leader who talked about his community work and its impact on people. He was outgunned, and though he was well accepted, he clearly was given less prominence and time than the first speaker.

At the second session, the speaker introduced a new counseling industry that helps workers keep prepared for moving into another position. Adaptation was the key theme and staying at the ready to change jobs by continually updating skills and resumé was the message. There was no counterbalancing presentation; it seemed to be assumed that the new work environment meant that workers were expendable.

The third and final presentation was on professional preparation and its usefulness in the marketplace. The major message here was to teach practical skills for a changing work environment. The places of critique, quality of life, and personal satisfaction were not discussed. The essence of these speakers, except for the community speaker in the first session, was about outsourcing, right-sizing, and portability of assets without any critique of the assumptions underlying these prescriptions. The market was in charge. There was one uncontested message at these scheduled general sessions: the job of adult education is preparing docile and technically capable workers for the workplace. Fortunately, the social philosophy speaker was able to challenge the biases and present alternative views to an affirming audience. If the social activists had not fought for the right to have a social philosophy session, the ideology of a market-driven philosophy would have been reified as the majority view.

Accordingly, the lack of position papers, the lack of encouraging debate in the presentations, and the scheduling of social philosophy speakers late in the conference were all ways of discouraging dialogue. This cultural reproduction of majority ideology leads to questions about knowledge and power and begs an examination of the nexus of these two political dimensions within the organization.

Knowledge and Power

Research is a process of developing and systematizing knowledge. In examining this systematizing process, critical questions include: Who does it?

For what purpose? Who gains and who loses? I believe that an association should encourage all its members to do intellectual work, to produce knowledge. This means engaging as a group in a critically reflective process, and when the association comes together on an annual basis, it should be an opportunity for all participants to report on their research, seek critique, and promote debate. The assumptions within this definition could provide guidance as to an association's activities and decision-making apparatus. My assumptions are these:

- All members of the association are potential intellectuals and are capable of creating knowledge.
- Theory and practice are inseparable, and knowledge is produced through praxis.
- There are many differing types of knowledge, and they compete for primacy through power relations.
- Reality is socially constructed and reconstructed and functions to perpetuate existing power relations.

If you accept these definitions and assumptions, then you will have to agree with me that AAACE has not for the most part been about doing, sharing, critiquing, or encouraging debate on knowledge generation. Nor has it had a vision that all members are potential intellectuals and capable of critical analyses. If anything, the association appears to suppress inquiry. The following evidence supports this view:

- AAACE has not systematically generated policy position papers or had an explicit mission statement for what it does or does not support.
- The endowment for the Houle award for scholarly writing was depleted as a result of poor stewardship. Furthermore, there have been too few awards to honor and promote research among academics and no awards for community researchers.
- The association staff had begun to censor scholarly activity, as illustrated in the saga of the *Making Space* book.

Some history is relevant here. In 1964, Jensen, Liveright, and Hallenbeck's *Adult Education: Outlines of an Emerging Field of University Study*, informally known as the black book, was published and set the direction for the field for the next two decades. In 1986, CPAE and AAACE approved a proposal for an updated version of the black book as a way of recognizing its twenty-fifth anniversary. The new book (now called the black and blue book) was severely criticized at the 1992 AERC annual meeting because, with the exception of chapters by two women, it left out the contributions and activity of marginalized groups (Carlson, 1992). The AERC membership voted, with one nay vote, to insist on a new book, sponsored by AAACE, that would be inclusive and not silence the many voices wanting to be heard. This new book (called the pink and purple book) was proposed by the CPAE and approved by the membership at the 1992 fall meeting. The editors were not selected until 1995, and in 1996 the AAACE association staff pulled the project, claiming little interest from publishers. Committed to carrying on the hard work by the African American and feminist groups to get the book sponsored and supported, the editors withdrew the book from the association and sought to publish it independently. The book was eventually developed through a participatory process, a publisher was readily found, and *Making Spaces* was born—but with no help from the association (Sissel and Sheared, forthcoming).

The controversy over the book goes deeper than it may seem. The contentious issues here were about knowledge and power. Why did the AERC become the place where the debate over inclusion takes place? I believe it was because the AERC is close to the ground, nonhierarchical, open, and inexpensive and encourages student attendance. Conversely, I believe the AAACE has become elitist, closed, expensive, and nonparticipatory. Following the book episode in 1992, some have not returned to the AERC because of its "leftist" politics. Other members have been active in developing another organization, the Academy of Human Resource Development (AHRD), which parallels the AERC but focuses on human resource development. Some of the social activist groups, though active in the AERC and CPAE, have helped form a progressive alliance, NAAPAE, under the umbrella of the International Council for Adult Education. The alliance favors a Freirean approach to practice and governs in a Freirean, highly participatory, if at times tedious, democratic mode.

Both organizations are different from AACE and AERC. The research paradigm most often used at the AHRD conference is positivism with statistical manipulation. The AERC substantially moved away from that paradigm in the 1980s and promotes, and may even favor, interpretive, historical, and philosophical inquiry. Some are concerned about a new hegemony (Carlson, 1992).

In contrast to the AAACE, the NAAPAE culture demands a low-priced, environmental-friendly, relaxed venue. Conference attendance is usually below three hundred. The agenda is built over several months by the constituents, with various groups contributing. There is a mix of popular education, reports on participatory research, and popular culture. In 1999, the Tucson, Arizona, conference featured First Nations cultural presentations; a canvas mural eight by twenty feet was painted by the participants on themes emerging from the small groups; music, art, and nature are emphasized. The connections made here are face-to-face and deep. For example, use of plastic plateware and vegetarian meals were issues democratically resolved by the participants. It is clear that these four organizations are expressing different values.

Successes

It is fair to note that the AAACE has had its successes; the terrain looks bleak, but no hegemony is complete. Here are some brighter spots:

- The Salt Lake City Convention in 1990 featured substantive debate, relevant programs, and First Lady Barbara Bush, who was involved in literacy.
- The AAACE 1993 publications committee published *Popular Education in Quebec* and *Freedom Road*.
- The *Adult Education Quarterly Journal* has maintained an extensive list of consulting editors, representing a broad ideological agenda.
- The International League for Social Justice movement was initiated in 1984 out of the CPAE by Hal Beder, leading to the development of Popular Education Institutes, currently held each summer at Rutgers, the State University of New Jersey.
- Counter-discourse initiatives (heterosexism, critical theory, feminism, critical pedagogy, human resource development critique and Africentric discourse) seem to start at the AERC and then permeate to the CPAE. Many of these discourses are reflected in the curriculum of various adult education graduate programs.
- The CPAE launched the transatlantic professional exchange between 1985 and 1988 and spun off the international preconference, now fully integrated into the AERC (Cunningham, 1991).
- The John McKnight debate on deprofessionalizing was initiated within the CPAE.

Clearly the CPAE and conference program leaders have provided a limited forum for debating some issues. The problem is twofold: the mechanisms for membership participation with the encouragement of debate are not present and the leadership to promote policy analyses from many standpoints has not been forthcoming.

Conclusion

The AAACE, with its umbrella concept, has been less than successful in satisfying its members. Those working in the trenches of literacy and welfare, work, and English as a Second Language want practical help with their practice and participatory decision making in the association; those in human resource development want an association that has as its goal learning for earning but focused on business and industry's bottom line; those who espouse learning for living desire an association with Juntos, and they tend to shun conflict and promote uncontested humanism; those who wish to build civil society and promote social justice want a democratic structure, a participatory body politic, and clearly defined social goals.

Each of these groups is so caught up in its ideologies that they cannot come together despite their conflicts and see that in our contemporary world, new unions must be forged and a democratic society starts with a democratic association. We can influence the larger society only if we demonstrate that we can work together in a conflictual world. The leadership to accomplish this negotiation has been lacking.

References

Adult Education Association. *AEA-USA Task Force Report on Voluntary Learning.* Washington, D.C.: Adult Education Association, 1981.

Adult Education Quarterly Editorial Board. "Requested Actions." Memo to the Board of Directors of the American Association for Adult and Continuing Education, Nov. 11, 1997.

Allbritton, D. "1997 State of the Association Report." Paper presented at the American Association for Adult and Continuing Education Conference, Cincinnati, Ohio, Nov. 1997.

American Association for Adult and Continuing Education. "AAACE Minutes of the General Membership/Annual Business Meeting." Charlotte, N.C., Nov. 1, 1996.

American Association for Adult and Continuing Education. "AAACE Galaxy Conference Report." Unpublished paper, 1999.

Carlson, R. "Open Season on Gatekeepers at the 1992 Adult Education Research Conference." *CPAE Newsletter,* Summer 1992.

Commission of Professors of Adult Education. "CPAE Treasurers Report, Annual Business Meeting." Nov. 18, 2000.

Cunningham, P. "International Influences on the Development of Knowledge." In J. Peters and P. Jarvis (eds.), *Adult Education: Evolution and Achievements in a Field of Study.* San Francisco: Jossey-Bass, 1991.

Cunningham, P. "United States of America." *International Review of Education: The Legislature and Policy Environment, UNESCO,* 1996, *40,* 1–3, 167–186.

Fingeret, A., and Jurmo, P. "Editors' Notes." In A. Fingeret and P. Jurmo (eds.), *Participatory Literacy Education.* New Directions for Continuing Education, no. 42. San Francisco: Jossey-Bass, 1989.

Jensen, G., Liveright, A. A., and Hallenbeck, W. *Adult Education: Outlines of an Emerging Field of University Study.* Chicago: Adult Education Association of the U.S.A., 1964.

McVey, B. "Treasurer's Report." Report presented at the American Association for Adult and Continuing Education Annual Business Meeting, Cincinnati, Ohio, Nov. 11, 1997.

Mezirow, J. "Faded Visions and Fresh Commitments: Adult Education's Social Goals." Policy paper prepared for the American Association for Adult and Continuing Education, Nov. 5, 1991.

Ohliger, J. "Reconciling Education with Liberty." *UNESCO Prospects,* 1983, *13,* 161–179.

Sheared, V., and Sissel, P. *Making Space: Reframing Practice in Adult Education.* Westport, Connecticut: Greenwood Publishing Group, 2001.

PHYLLIS M. CUNNINGHAM is Activist Scholar in adult education at Northern Illinois University, DeKalb.

8

Traditionally, the profession of adult education has been defined in terms of applied technical expertise. This chapter proposes expanding that definition by forging occupational alliances, becoming reflective practitioners, and engaging more politically.

Professionalization: A Politics of Identity

Arthur L. Wilson

For decades, there has been discussion about how adult education could improve its identity and power as a profession (Houle, 1991). As with most other occupations, the common response since the 1920s has been to portray adult education as an applied technical profession defined by rigorous scientific investigation. Debate topics center around whether this is the right approach, whether adult education is better thought of as a vocation, whether it is scientific at all, and so on. My sense is that the attempt to adopt an applied technical science framework has not worked particularly well because it does not adequately portray significant dimensions of our work. Furthermore, following on the sociology of the professions, a central problem in constituting professional identity is one of controlling access to and training for the profession. Adult education to date has been unable to achieve the training and occupational monopoly that constitutes the professional identity of more successful professions, nor is it likely to do so in the near future. Thus, in my view, the question remains, On what grounds are we to construct a professional identity in adult education?

Questions of access and control are essentially political in that they are about structuring professional relations of power. Given such a politics of identity, how should we respond? I argue for three strategies to build our identities as adult educators. First, we have to link our adult education expertise professionally with numerous other professional and occupational groups that depend significantly on adult education practices. Second, we must move away from a blind adherence to technical forms of adult education to engage in a much more forthright reflective practice. Third, in moving toward reflective practice, we must make clear the political and ethical consequences that

NEW DIRECTIONS FOR ADULT AND CONTINUING EDUCATION, no. 91, Fall 2001   © John Wiley & Sons, Inc.

are too often shrouded by our focus on the technical aspects of our work. I argue in the end that we must ask clearer questions and provide better answers about who our work benefits and why.

Living in the Past: The False Hope of Technical Rationality

To understand where we might be and could possibly be going, it may be helpful to look a bit at where we have been. It is my sense that the field of adult and continuing education, both its practitioners and scholars, has generally but largely uncritically adopted a particular professionalization ideology, one intended to produce a specific professional identity, from the very beginnings of organized, professional adult education in the United States in the 1920s. An integrated accounting of this ideological movement and production of identity in adult and continuing education over time needs creating, yet there are many selective and tantalizing insights into its history and progression. (For a general sense of the story as well as some introduction to the different interpretations, see Brookfield, 1989; Galbraith and Zelenak, 1989; Houle, 1992; Jensen, Liveright, and Hallenbeck, 1964; Knowles, 1960; Peters and others, 1991; Podeschi, 2000; Welton, 1987; Wilson, 1993; Wilson and Cervero, 1997).

Schön (1983) provides one of the better characterizations of this ideology of professionalization and identity in this often-cited definition of *technical rationality:* "Professional activity consists in instrumental problem solving made rigorous by the application of scientific theory and technique" (p. 21). Over the decades, adult education scholars have relentlessly attempted to define professional identity within this strictly drawn definition of professional activity. Through such efforts, adult and continuing education has become uniformly understood as an applied professional field (modeled on medicine and engineering) as it became increasingly focused on elaborating procedural responses to practical problems. As Cunningham (1989) remarked, the "means" have been defined as "ends," as we pursued questions of what Lindeman (1926) long ago warned us to avoid: technical or "mechanical" overspecialization in what he and many others have believed is better understood as a social and cultural practice rather than a scientific one.

What does "instrumental problem solving made rigorous by science" mean exactly? A bit of the story might help here. In my view, there is a pervasive faith in American cultural and professional life, running back before the Industrial Revolution, that scientific investigation will provide reliable solutions to the human and social problems that beset us (see Kett, 1994, for how this plays out in adult education in the nineteenth century). Thus, in the context of how occupations professionalize, it is generally an unchallenged precept that one major definer of how successful an occupation is in professionalizing depends on how scientific it can define its practice

(Flexner, 1915; Larson, 1979; Schön, 1983). As Moore (1970, p. 56) noted, "Professionals . . . apply very generalized principles, standardized knowledge, to concrete problems." Examples abound: medicine, engineering, the military, and so on.

The largely middle-class manifestations of adult education emerged as a professionalizing endeavor during the peak of this movement and, not surprisingly, has been carried along with it. A set of common concerns, which we would think of as practice principles today, were inchoately announced in 1948 (Wilson, 1993). These concerns actually have clear origins in association and university professionalizing endeavors to study and define adult education in the 1920s and 1930s. The movement to define the practice of adult education in instrumental ways, despite vociferous and often acrid objections by a professorial minority in recent years, continues largely unabated today, with a plethora of publications, conferences, and professional training programs all purporting to "improve practice" by teaching "scientific" knowledge about how adults learn and the "professional" techniques for organizing, delivering, and evaluating how adults learn.

The false hope is the presumption that this applied science understanding accounts fully for what adult and continuing-education practice actually entails. I have no doubt that the procedural emphases, whose impetus emerges from both scholars and practitioners alike, are indeed quite central to our actual educational work and worth. Assessing needs, designing instruction, planning programs, evaluating efforts, and the various other procedural activities are part of our professional identity by virtue of the execution and effectiveness of our expertise. The problem is in attempting to define professional work so unilaterally. I want to use this background to the professional identity question to make the following distinction. Aristotle began a conversation that has undergone significant discussion ever since (Bernstein, 1983), although its merit has largely been lost in the century of science that we have just lived through. Aristotle noted that certain kinds of knowledge are good for making things; such knowledge has come to be known as technical competence in the way just described and is thus very useful in understanding how to do things. He elaborated that the knowledge necessary to make the right choices about what to do (not just how) was practical, not technical. Practical knowledge has to do with acting correctly in a moral and political sense, not just a skills-based sense, as is the thrust of instrumental professional work. Technical knowledge is relatively useless for informing the moral and political dilemmas that we face in daily practice. As often noted (Briton, 1996; Cunningham, 1989; Welton, 1987, 1995), adult educators are typically "obsessed" with "how" questions and too often insouciant with "what for" questions. Thus, the importance of this distinction between technical and practical for (re)constructing our professional identity lies in endeavoring to (re)claim the moral and political dimensions of our work.

Are We or Are We Not a Profession?

The problem of constructing professional identity has not gone unnoticed in adult education (Cervero, 1987). The ideology of professionalization defined as scientifically based technical practice, which in turn becomes the identifier and thus identity of professional educational work, emerged more than a hundred years ago (Flexner, 1915). This dominant position has remained unreflectively articulated as the rationale for graduate program development, research, and professional training since the 1930s. For example, every handbook on adult education since 1934 has had a chapter on training practitioners, all of which depend on the instrumental logic of technical rationality. This dominant position has not gone unquestioned, however. Houle's concern with this question has long standing. Although the author of many publications on adult education leadership training and unabashedly a proponent of a scientific approach to adult education, he nonetheless had a keen sense of the demands of actual practice in a practical, not solely technical way (Houle, 1972). Although there has been ongoing anxiety about such a limited professional identity (see Lindeman, 1926), serious questions began arising again in the 1980s. In that regard, Cervero's (1988) and Nowlen's (1988) work on continuing professional education, built on the groundbreaking revelations of Schön (1983), began to crack the ideological facade of the scientifically based technical movement. A culminating moment came in the early 1990s when Collins (1992) argued that adult education should resist further professionalization and constitute itself as a "committed pedagogy" dedicated to an explicit political agenda that places emancipatory interests above professionalizing ones. Cervero (1992) countered that professionalization was largely unstoppable but that the question still was open as to how to constitute our professional identity in terms of restructuring our relationships with learners and institutions.

The critique of adult education's simplistic understanding of theory-practice relationships, its overreliance on process over product, and its steadfast avowal of neutrality, all in the name of scientific objectivity, has a well-established history (for example, see Briton, 1996; Brookfield, 1989; Welton, 1987, 1995) and needs no great rehearsing here. The point I am making is not only that technical rationality has helped produce our dominant but weak notions of theory-practice relations and thus impoverished our actual practical work; it has also helped to construct a weak professional identity, one that continues to disadvantage our practical work as well as our institutional standing. I believe that it is no historical accident, for example, that various adult education professional associations have collapsed periodically, which I believe partially results from a lack of any substantial professional identity. Trying to corral the amorphous professional identity of the adult education enterprise can be likened to popular adages such as herding cats or nailing gelatin to a tree. Unlike other professions whose identity the public perceives as established, coherent, and purposeful (rarely does the public really see the conflict, fragmentation, and dissolution that characterize nearly all professions), adult and continuing education has little publicly understood professional identity. Our attempts to legitimate ourselves professionally—that is, define our identity—through scientific rigor have not helped significantly in establishing that identity. Cervero (1992) countered that professionalization was largely unstoppable but that the question still was open as to how to constitute our professional identity in terms of restructuring our relationships with learners and institutions.

One way to understand this failure is to use a different way to see the problem. It may not simply be a problem of not meeting standards of scientific legitimacy. The failure to construct a recognizable professional identity could also be a problem of access and control that is tied to constructing effective relations of professional power. Larson (1979) has demonstrated that it is not just the production of scientific knowledge and development of techniques that defines a profession. Professional identity also requires the profession to be able to control who produces professional knowledge, who has access to that knowledge, and how they use it. By controlling the production, access, and use of professional knowledge, professions can thus monopolize the market for their services (all successful professions have done this). Producing a recognizable professional commodity means producing a professional trained in discipline-specific knowledge and skill who, as the only available purveyor, can "sell" that expertise in the professional marketplace. Specific academic credentials, qualifying exams, licenses, certification, and other restrictive measures that entitle only a select few to practice typically structure such monopolization. Thus, only licensed nurses can practice nursing, licensed engineers practice engineering, and so on. Controlling the market is essential to constructing professional power—that is, capacity to act—which then produces a specific professional identity. Cervero (1992) countered that professionalization was largely unstoppable but that the question still was open as to how to constitute our professional identity in terms of restructuring our relationships with learners and institutions.

Cervero (1987, 1988) first introduced Larson's analysis from the sociology of professions in his study of continuing professional education. But it would appear that we have yet to gain any insights from such analysis. This does not mean that there have not been attempts to monopolize the production of knowledge and practice of adult education (Cervero, 1987; Galbraith and Zelenak, 1989); clearly, this has been an agenda for graduate training programs since the 1930s (Houle, 1991). Another example is the intermittent discussion in the 1970s and 1980s about whether, how, and whom to certify as adult education practitioners (it is often the role of professional associations to test, certify, and thus control access to a specific occupation). But adult education remains unruly, indeed often unrecognizable (consider the variety of reactions when introducing yourself to others as an adult educator). And even more important, anyone can do it. Historical and contemporary evidence profoundly demonstrates just how open the doors are to the practice of adult education. It seems to make almost no difference whether one has professional training and knowledge, at least in terms of being allowed to do adult education (it may also make no difference in the quality of work itself whether one has professional training and knowledge). The point in terms of creating professional identity is that by not being able to constitute and service a market for who we are and what we do, we therefore are not able to create any sort of recognizable professional identity. That is not to say there is no market for what we purport to do, just that we do not control access to it or knowledge about it.

To steal a phrase, our inability to control access and market results in an identity crisis. Just who are we, and why don't our long-standing prescriptions for practice (the supposedly scientific rigor that stipulates our theory and practice) work to define our identity? This is not a new crisis. It just seems that way. It is my sense that we have struggled with this question since the 1926 founding of the American Association for Adult Education, which coincided dramatically with Lindeman's 1926 warning to avoid the very thing we have spent the past seventy-five years searching for: a professional occupation defined by specialized knowledge and technique. So what is at stake in such an identity crisis? The rewards and losses have been well rehearsed elsewhere (Cervero, 1987, 1988, 1992; Collins, 1992; Galbraith and Zelenak, 1989). What concerns me more is the sense of worth and ability (as well as energy) tied up in such continuing crises. It may be that a professionalized practice of adult education really has little to contribute to the substantive endeavors of adults learning. If so, let the erosion of our graduate training programs continue, let the co-optation of adult education by the rhetoric and reality of lifelong learning continue, let our own professional invisibility continue, and maybe by our own professional centennial we can go out of business.

The Politics of Identity

Of course, that is not going to happen, at least not right away. There are lots of people who self-identify as adult educators, and institutions routinely ask for and expect us to provide our services and expertise. While it may be an open question as to how well graduate programs are doing or what they are accomplishing, we are participating to some extent in the makeover of adult education into lifelong learning, which is something we should have something to say about. To do so, to continue to be adult educators, perhaps even to thrive rather than be professionally invisible, we have to construct a professional identity that is not just technically sophisticated but is also politically astute and ethically informed (Cervero and Wilson, 1994). I propose three aspects of professional identity to consider in constructing a more formidable professional presence able to contribute significantly to adult learning endeavors: first, we must form occupational alliances with other professions; second, we should expand our rather myopic focus on technical forms of adult education to become more reflective practitioners; and third, we must recognize our work as a cultural practice with specific political and ethical intentions. I propose these positions not conclusively but as starting points for escaping the entrapment of a technical past as well as a way of embracing our historical successes at negotiating political and moral dilemmas by sometimes being on the right side at the right time.

Forge Professional Alliances. The pursuit of technical efficiency was a course of action set in motion early in the twentieth century and has varied little since. In attempting to define identity through professional specialization, earlier adult educators colonized knowledge about how adults learn as our subject expertise and the production of opportunities for adult learning as our technical expertise. This has been a very important accomplishment and should in no way be minimized, for without them, we have no starting points in crafting professional identity. The problem resides, however, in the very dimension that makes adult learning such an enticing endeavor. As often noted, its ubiquity makes it inconceivably difficult to contain. Once one catches sight of what it means for adults to learn, then the phenomenon can be found almost anywhere. While wondrous, it defies the sort of professional monopolizing that Larson (1979) suggested. My sense is that the calculus for producing professional adult educators is missing some significant elements that would make for a more visible professional identity.

So here is the proposal. We must link our expertise and technical skills to other professional bodies of knowledge and skills. Borrowing Anthony Giddens's notion of the duality of structure, I propose that adult educators more actively pursue what seems to be a regular but not so obvious occurrence in the graduate preparation of adult educators: a duality of professions. We must link our adult education expertise with the numerous other professional and occupational endeavors that depend significantly on adult education practices but typically do not see themselves as "doing" education. I think a stronger professional identity can be forged by deliberately connecting adult education expertise with nursing, human resources, extension, radiology, lawyers, architects, the ministry, and so on. Rather than trying to identify ourselves as experts in a generic notion of adults and learning, we need to produce educators who have expertise in adult education and some other professional context. For example, nurses working with adult learners in patient education or continuing professional education for nurses need to have both nursing training and adult education training. Professional identity thus is constituted by training and practice in a professional field and training and practice in adult education. Frequently, I have worked with diploma-, baccalaureate-, or master's-level registered nurses who are seeking master's or doctoral degrees in adult education because their work is as much about adult education as it is about nursing. Such a duality of professional expertise creates a recognizable professional identity that represents both specific contents and processes. It escapes the professional dead end in adult education where we purvey expertise in learning processes but represent no particular subject competency.

Develop Reflective Practice. There is no doubt that our professional identity requires technical skills. This is not an argument to ignore that dimension but to say that the demands and challenges of real practice go beyond technical skill mastery. As is well established in many professions (Cervero, 1988; Schön, 1983), it is not technical rigor but judgmental acuity that demarcates novice, from competent, from superlative practitioner. Such judgments do not simply emulate procedural cannons for solving problems; they represent complex interplays of individual and organizational beliefs, assumptions, values, experiences, training, and intentions, which Nowlen (1988) described as the double helix of practice. As has been pointed out over and over, professional practice is not just a matter of solving previously encountered problems; it is as much and more about seeing what the problems are, how they differ from case to case, and what constitutes the uniqueness of each case the practitioner faces (Schön, 1983). Furthermore, there are special conditions that define the nature of professional practice, which technical rigor is unable to address effectively by itself. The contemporary conditions of professional practice include growing technological complexity, knowledge explosions and disappearances, increasing systemic delivery of professional services and concomitant loss of individual autonomy, escalating overspecialization with a loss of coordination and integration, overreliance on ineffective theoretical frameworks, ineffective continuing education (mandatory or otherwise), escalating practitioner obsolescence, and increasing risk as a function of increasing uncertainty with respect to conflicting professional analyses (Cervero, 1988; Wilson and Hayes, 2000). Again, it is now a long-standing but still little understood or well-heeded argument that professional practice is not just technical but also judgmental and highly constrained contextually. So it is unreasonable to expect that rigorous instrumental problem solving and technical rationality can well manage what we know to be the complex demands and conditions of modern professional practice.

There is evidence that as professionals develop into exemplary practitioners, reflection plays an important developmental role (Mott and Daley, 2000). But as several chapter authors in the Mott and Daley book suggest, we cannot afford just to expect reflective practitioners to somehow develop; we have to inculcate a reflective dimension to professional training, whether it be collegial, conference, or graduate learning. It is my sense that there has been some movement to incorporate a reflective dimension in professional graduate training. But it certainly is not systematic yet, and the technical emphasis is quite persistent and resistant to change (as any perusal of professional training publications will quickly attest). My obvious proposal is to move away from a blind adherence to technical forms of adult education, shed our false and disingenuous faith in process above product, and engage in a much more forthright reflective practice. And we must do it philosophically, practically, and systemically throughout our professional training efforts. The value of such a move is not just to account for the complex exigencies of daily practice but to get beyond the "how to" in order to address the "what for."

Practice Politics. In moving toward reflective (as opposed to solely technical) practice, we must make the politics of our practice serve the politics of our identity. This requires a political and ethical commitment to determining who typically does benefit from adult education in order to determine and serve those who typically do not benefit from adult education. We should be asking hard questions about who our work benefits; too often, we do not. In the quest for professional identity, adult education has remained largely a middle-class phenomenon focused on benefiting those already well positioned. We have a rich history and much contemporary work that challenges the socially reproductive adult education that many of us are engaged in. As Cervero and Wilson (2001) recently argued, we can no longer afford the professed innocence of our past in which our chief professional pursuit was to "romance the adult learner." We now know more than ever before that adult education is deeply involved in the struggle for knowledge and power in society. As Cervero and I have tried to show, there is a reciprocal relationship between the production of power and the role of adult education in the production of power; the larger social structures of inequitable distributions of material and symbolic resources are played out in and through adult education. We cannot escape our complicity in such distributions by claiming ignorance, feigning neutrality, or, worse, professing technical competence. Asking the question of who is benefiting from our actions is a way of understanding the politics of our work. Asking the question of who should benefit is a way of understanding the ethics of our work. As we have argued, "There is no politically innocent place for adult educators. At the heart of practice, then, we must clearly understand that every adult educator is a social activist" (Cervero and Wilson, 2001, p. 13) whose work directly affects who benefits from the production and distribution of power. There are other specifics to understanding these broad claims, such as how we understand our responsibilities for our actions and the particular position we inhabit as "knowledge-power brokers." Suffice it to say for this discussion of identity politics that our professional identity requires us to engage directly with this essential question of benefits. By taking sides, by being explicit about whom we represent and why, we make clear the political and ethical dimensions of our identity. We become visible by standing clearly for something.

Parting Reflections

The editors of this volume are seeking to contribute to, as well as make more visible, what adult and continuing educators already know a lot about but rarely discuss in public: the politics of our work. I have witnessed much of the past decade's discussion about what the politics of our work looks like, how we can better understand our practice as political activity, and what the ethical positions and consequences of such engagement should or could look like. What I have tried to sketch here is that the politics of our work is intimately caught up in the politics of our identity. Adult educators are no longer free to imagine their neutrality, try as they might to continue to do so. If we are ever to establish a formidable professional identity rather than wither away, we must enlarge our classical understandings of how to constitute our professional identity to embrace broader understandings of what our work looks like and what is really at stake when we practice adult education.

References

Bernstein, R. *Beyond Objectivism and Relativism*. Philadelphia: University of Pennsylvania, 1983.

Briton, D. *The Modern Practice of Adult Education: A Postmodern Critique*. Albany: State University of New York Press, 1996.

Brookfield, S. "The Epistemology of Adult Education in the United States and Great Britain: A Cross-Cultural Analysis." In B. Bright (ed.), *The Epistemological Imperative*. London: Croom Helm, 1989.

Cervero, R. "Professionalization as an Issue for Continuing Education." In R. Brockett (ed.), *Continuing Education in the Year 2000*. New Directions for Continuing Education, no. 36. San Francisco: Jossey-Bass, 1987.

Cervero, R. *Effective Continuing Education for Professionals*. San Francisco: Jossey-Bass, 1988.

Cervero, R. "Becoming More Effective in Everyday Practice." In A. Quigley (ed.), *Fulfilling the Promise of Adult and Continuing Education*. New Directions for Continuing Education, no. 44. San Francisco: Jossey-Bass, 1989.

Cervero, R. "Adult and Continuing Education Should Strive for Professionalization." In M. Galbraith and B. Sisco (eds.), *Confronting Controversies in Challenging Times: A Call for Action*. New Directions for Adult and Continuing Education, no. 54. San Francisco: Jossey-Bass, 1992.

Cervero, R., and Wilson, A. *Planning Responsibly for Adult Education: A Guide to Negotiating Power and Interests*. San Francisco: Jossey-Bass, 1994.

Cervero, R., and Wilson, A. (eds.). *Power in Practice: Adult Education and the Struggle for Knowledge and Power in Society*. San Francisco: Jossey-Bass, 2001.

Collins, M. "Adult and Continuing Education Should Resist Further Professionalization." In M. Galbraith and B. Sisco (eds.), *Confronting Controversies in Challenging Times: A Call for Action*. New Directions for Adult and Continuing Education, no. 54. San Francisco: Jossey-Bass, 1992.

Cunningham, P. "Making a More Significant Impact on Society." In B. A. Quigley (ed.), *Fulfilling the Promise of Adult and Continuing Education*. New Directions for Continuing Education, no. 44. San Francisco: Jossey-Bass, 1989.

Flexner, A. "Is Social Work a Profession?" *School and Society*, 1915, *1*, 901–911.

Galbraith, M., and Zelenak, G. "The Education of Adult and Continuing Education Practitioners." In S. Merriam and P. Cunningham (eds.), *Handbook of Adult and Continuing Education*. San Francisco: Jossey-Bass, 1989.

Houle, C. *The Design of Education*. San Francisco: Jossey-Bass, 1972.

Houle, C. "Foreword." In J. Peters, P. Jarvis, and Associates, *Adult Education*. San Francisco: Jossey-Bass, 1991.

Houle, C. *The Literature of Adult Education.* San Francisco: Jossey-Bass, 1992.

Jensen, G., Liveright, A., and Hallenbeck, W. (eds.). *Adult Education: Outlines of an Emerging Field of University Study.* Chicago: Adult Education Association of the U.S.A., 1964.

Kett, J. *The Pursuit of Knowledge Under Difficulties.* Stanford, Calif.: Stanford University, 1994.

Knowles, M. (ed.). *Handbook of Adult Education in the US.* Chicago: Adult Education Association, 1960.

Larson, M. *The Rise of Professionalism.* Berkeley: University of California Press, 1979.

Lindeman, E. *The Meaning of Adult Education.* New York: New Republic, 1926.

Moore, W. *The Professions: Roles and Rules.* New York: Russell Sage Foundation, 1970.

Mott, V., and Daley, B. (eds.). *Charting a Course for Continuing Professional Education: Reframing Professional Practice.* New Directions for Adult and Continuing Education, no. 86. San Francisco: Jossey-Bass, 2000.

Nowlen, P. *A New Approach to Continuing Education for Business and the Professions.* Old Tappan, N.J.: Macmillan, 1988.

Peters, J., Jarvis, P., and Associates. *Adult Education: Evolution and Achievements in a Developing Field of Study.* San Francisco: Jossey-Bass, 1991.

Podeschi, R. "Evolving Directions in Professionalization and Philosophy." In A. L. Wilson and E. R. Hayes (eds.), *Handbook of Adult and Continuing Education.* San Francisco: Jossey-Bass, 2000.

Schön, D. *The Reflective Practitioner.* New York: Basic Books, 1983.

Welton, M. "'Vivisecting the Nightengale': Reflections on Adult Education as an Object of Study." *Studies in the Education of Adults,* 1987, 19, 46–68.

Welton, M. (ed.). *In Defense of the Lifeworld.* Albany: State University of New York Press, 1995.

Wilson, A. "The Common Concern: Controlling the Professionalization of Adult Education." *Adult Education Quarterly,* 1993, 44, 1–16.

Wilson, A., and Cervero, R. "The Song Remains the Same: The Selective Tradition of Technical Rationality in Adult Education Program Planning Theory." *International Journal of Lifelong Education,* 1997, 18, 84–108.

Wilson, A. L., and Hayes, E. R. "On Thought and Action in Adult and Continuing Education." In A. L. Wilson and E. Hayes (eds.), *Handbook of Adult and Continuing Education.* San Francisco: Jossey-Bass, 2000.

ARTHUR L. WILSON *is associate professor of adult education in the Department of Education at Cornell University, Ithaca, New York.*

9

This chapter examines selected issues from previous chapters to create a picture of the political landscape of adult education. Strategies for negotiating the landscape of adult education are suggested and discussed.

The Political Landscape of Adult Education: From the Personal to Political and Back Again

Catherine A. Hansman

Several years ago, I was program coordinator of the Center for Women and Returning Adults at a midwestern university. In that role, I found myself quickly submerged in a swirl of politics as I attempted to champion issues important to both women and adult learners in higher education. The political issues surrounding physical space, restricted funding, and limited academic programs and student services bound my efforts to develop programs. The reasons for this were many. First, the Center for Women and Returning Adults was not a center—and certainly not central to the campus. Instead, the "center" was a small office buried in the basement of a building very much removed from the main activities of the campus. Second, with a part-time secretary as my only staff, we were hard pressed to serve the population of women and adult students who needed the counseling and other services we offered. Third, the program budget for the center was less than four thousand dollars a year, thus effectively limiting the types of programs I could plan and offer for women and adult learners. Fourth, although the university was a commuter campus and the student population was composed of more than half adult learners, the academic programs and student service organizations organized themselves around the needs of a younger traditional-age learner. Finally, the center was hampered—financially, physically, and programmatically—by the politics surrounding the perception that only "poor" women would use it and that "real" (read white, middle class, and/or male) returning adult students had no need of the services we offered. Thus, funding and other resources were limited and generally

NEW DIRECTIONS FOR ADULT AND CONTINUING EDUCATION, no. 91, Fall 2001 © John Wiley & Sons, Inc.

unsupported, and programs that were approved were perceived by administration to uphold the traditional roles of women (as wife, mother).

I wish I could say that I was able to negotiate the political turf in that university and provide many helpful programs for both women and returning adults, but I cannot. My major accomplishment while in that position was helping to establish a campus day care center, perceived by administration as a traditional "women's need" (although fathers signed up their children in equal numbers to mothers). I was able to accomplish this feat only through concerted political maneuvering. This entailed having a thorough understanding of the political landscape on that campus and how to negotiate it. The day care center undoubtedly benefited both women and returning students (and faculty and staff, who were also allowed to use it), but it was supported, while other programs with less mainstream goals were not. I was a political player, and I tried to be aware, but was not always sure, of what game was being played.

With apologies to Shakespeare, in whatever role we play as adult educators, we are but actors and all the world is a political stage, one that is perhaps defined by "wider systems of social, economic, and cultural relations of power" (Cervero and Wilson, 2001, p. 6). But perhaps the stage is set for a plurality of new voices to be heard (Aronowitz and Giroux, 1991). As the chapter authors in this volume have so richly described, the political realities of working within adult education surround us and cannot be ignored. This volume attempts to address some of these political issues and has focused on politics in adult education from a variety of perspectives: the political aspects of literacy education (Allan Quigley and Barbara Sparks); higher education (Peggy Sissel, Catherine Hansman, and Carol Kasworm); graduate adult education programs within colleges of education (Michael Day, Donna Amstutz, and Donna Whitson), achieving democracy in graduate classrooms and programs (Scipio A. J. Colin III and Tom Heaney); professional organizations as policymakers (Phyllis Cunningham); and the identity of adult educators (Arthur Wilson).

The Political Landscape Explored

My coeditor and I do not pretend to have given voice to all of the current political issues and turmoil within the field. Nevertheless, we hope that this volume will facilitate continuing discourse concerning these issues. Here I highlight and discuss some of the political issues presented by the chapter authors in the hope of creating understandings of political strategies for negotiating the political landscape of adult education.

What Identity? Wilson (Chapter Eight) contends that adult education suffers from an identity crisis. However timely political discussions are concerning the politics surrounding adult education identity, in reality political concerns in adult education are not new and encompass many areas within the field. One needs only to look at the chapter titles in tables of contents from past *Adult and Continuing Education Handbooks* (reprinted in Wilson and Hayes, 2000) to discover many of the issues of the past that continue to emerge and reemerge as burning unanswered questions and concerns. For instance, the 1936 handbook contains a chapter entitled, "How Shall We Conceive the Task of Adult Education?" The 1948 handbook opening chapter is titled, "What We Mean by Adult Education?" and among the first chapters in the 1960 handbook are, "What Is Adult Education?" and "The Function and Place of Adult Education in American Society." Similar chapters also appear in the 1989 *Handbook of Adult and Continuing Education:* "The Social Context of Adult and Continuing Education," "Defining Adult and Continuing Education," and "Purposes and Philosophies of Adult Education." The most recent handbook continues this trend with chapters such as "Adult Education and Society," "A Sociology of Adult Education," and "Evolving Directions in Professionalization and Philosophy."

Clearly, as the titles and contents of these handbooks chapters suggest, the political landscape of adult education centers around what exactly is our identity as adult educators. Is it adult basic education and literacy (ABLE) and general educational development educators and administrators, human resource development training professionals, higher education faculty and administration, health care professionals, or other identities? Perhaps the answer to this question begins with exploration of power and the "For whom? Who plans? Who benefits? For what purpose? Who decides?" questions (Cunningham, 1989; Deshler and Grudens-Schuck, 2000). These are inherently political questions; deciding who benefits from the content of programs is the essence of political thought and action in all areas of adult education; thus, this inquiry should be instigated by all adult educators, regardless of their form of practice. Wilson (Chapter Eight) argues that "the politics of our work is intimately caught up in the politics of our identity" and that "professional identity does require us to engage directly with this essential question of benefits. . . . By being explicit about whom we represent and why, we make clear the political and ethical dimensions of our identity." Heaney (2000) agrees, reasoning that "individual practitioners do not define the field of adult education, nor do experts. A definition of a field of practice is the social product of many individuals who negotiate the value and meaning of work they come to see as serving a common purpose over time" (p. 561).

But where is this negotiation of identity and definition of our work? If the lack of these discussions at recent American Association for Adult and Continuing Education (AAACE) meetings is any indication, it seems that we are stuck in a quagmire of conflicted identity. However, the time has come for us to negotiate differences and to develop and maintain our professional friendships and cross-border relationships within adult education while respecting the philosophical pluralism (Podeschi, 2000) that abounds in the field. Wilson recommends three actions to be taken in order to construct a formidable professional presence: form occupational alliances (for instance, with nursing, pharmacy, or law), become more reflective practitioners, and recognize the work of adult educators as a cultural practice with specific cultural and ethical intentions. These actions are clearly not ends but ideas to begin to clarify our identity as adult educators.

Professional Organizations. It seems that some of these discussions concerning identity should take place at meetings of our professional organizations. Cunningham (Chapter Seven) points out that our umbrella professional organization, the AAACE, has not respected cultural or philosophical pluralism and, indeed, seems to have taken actions that directly or indirectly have reduced the organization's capacity. Furthermore, AAACE has not been proactive politically in lobbying for adult education legislation or policies for the public good. Cunningham contends, "We lobby for jobs, not for effecting educational policy. We lobby through experts; we do not bring our members as intellectuals to the table to debate issues. . . . In summary, the membership was not engaged in educating their legislators or deciding what the goal of the policy development was to be." Cunningham is not alone in voicing her concern. Imel, Brockett, and James (2000) concur with Cunningham and list their anxieties about AAACE: unclear definition of purpose, splintering interests, inadequate funding, lack of interest in social issues, political inactivity, lack of vision, and elitism.

So what are the answers to the political swamp that AAACE finds itself, thus pulling its membership onto dangerous quicksand? As Cunningham contends, AAACE's umbrella concept of sheltering all areas has failed, although it has provided the space for those who identify within the field of adult education to meet. In order to save the organization, AAACE must encourage open debate among members about the means, goals, and purposes of the various factions of adult education (in other words, provide the space for identity discussions and actions). In addition, ideological space is needed for social action and leadership (from among members) to promote policy analysis and legislative action. Finally, it is crucial that the AAACE contribute to the development of the field through supporting and sponsoring research and scholarship, allowing discourse among members concerning policy issues, and becoming politically active regarding adult education legislation.

Are We Renting or Buying? Existing in Colleges of Education. Professional identity is also an issue in adult education graduate programs that reside in colleges of education at universities, which may result in tension among college of education colleagues. As Day, Amstutz, and Whitson (Chapter Four) declare, "During the more than seventy years of existence as an academic discipline in the United States, the field of adult education has spent a great deal of time examining itself as both an emerging and distinct field of study. . . . Central to this argument was the articulation of differences between their adult educational practices and that of other educators." This articulation resulted in tensions surrounding beliefs about knowledge, schools, learning, teaching, and resource allocation that has made problematic, in many cases, the existence of graduate adult education within colleges of education. Instead of reacting to these tensions from an unyielding stance or through isolating adult education departments and programs, Day, Amstutz, and Whitson suggest a perspective of compromise that challenges graduate adult education faculty to find ways to contribute to the missions of colleges of education. From their description of their own experiences in their graduate programs, they, as well as the entire College of Education at the University of Wyoming, have benefited from such compromises.

Literacy Education: Feudal Farmers and Peasant Wives. Just as issues surrounding identity are central to professional organizations and graduate education within adult education, the politics of democratic negotiation within literacy education is key to its survival. Sparks (Chapter Five) eloquently argues that "daily life is organized through policy, gender, race, and class . . . constructed in ways that spotlight conservative backlash against many of the social, economic, and political gains made by women, the poor, and people of color since the 1980s." She maintains that Title II of the Workforce Investment Act "seeks to control the domestic space of women, . . . singularly defines women as parents, and . . . women's literacy education has been reduced to women's roles as parent." Quigley (Chapter Six) realistically and poignantly examines literacy educators and likens their lives to the lives of farmers in the feudal era, arguing that "after centuries of democracy in North America, we live in inherited feudalistic system of direct and indirect controls over the politics and pedagogy of ABLE." His description of the day-to-day lives of literacy teachers and administrators and how public policy shapes the way programs are planned, funded, and executed shows how "new" political negotiation is essential to the survival of these programs. He accurately labels the entrenched "beyond-our-reach" thinking that hampers the politics of negotiating ABLE legislation.

Both Sparks and Quigley, while painting a bleak picture of the current state of ABLE and family literacy programs, describe in political terms the actions that need to take place in order for change to occur within literacy education. Quigley has already seen some political questions, discussions, and calls for action on the National Institute for Literacy (NIFL) listserv. This electronic discussion allowed all with computers and modems to participate and voice their concerns; thus, voices were heard from the "collective identity of the field," which, as Quigley notes, cannot be ignored in a democratic society. Quigley also argues for practitioner-based action research and reflection as a way of democratizing political discussion concerning literacy education. In similar fashion, Sparks pushes for feminist research and reexamination of educational policy that forces competing interests between women's development for parenting and women's development for work. Clearly, these are actions that will require the active participation and political action of literacy educators.

Democracy in Higher Education. Colin and Heaney (Chapter Three) ask, "Is democracy possible in the context of higher education?" They answer their own question by stating that adult education practice within higher education frequently ignores the democratic ideals of the field. In order to create a democratic practice, they argue, adult educators must operate politically amid contradictory and hegemonic institutions that require "balancing and negotiating power among groups that embody diverse cultural and gendered norms" and recognition of the "inequities of race, gender, and class . . . deeply embedded in institutional claims and functions of the university." Sissel, Hansman, and Kasworm (Chapter Two) also address the ways that universities ignore the needs of adult learners, contending that adult learners in higher educational settings are neglected in terms of public policy, programming, and mission, resulting in a lack of privilege, physical space, resources, and advocacy, and leading to marginalization of adult learners in higher education.

Given the arguments raised in the previous paragraph, is democracy possible within higher education? While a simple no may seem like the appropriate answer, Colin and Heaney detail the ways in which they are able to create and lead graduate programs and classes in adult education democratically. Central to their democratic practice is providing adult learners with opportunities for "articulation and analysis of multiple sociocultural experiences" and confronting issues of "intellectual imperialism and conceptual colonialism." This includes making space for scholars who have womanist, Africentric, feminist, and critical perspectives in their classrooms and their graduate programs. Consequently, a primary goal of their graduate programs is to encourage their doctoral students to emerge from the programs as change agents, committed to "facilitating a shift in power within the context of their respective practices" of adult education. Through balancing and negotiating power among differing and competing groups, cohort group learning, and peer relationships, Colin and Heaney describe political awareness and democratic strategies in action.

For adult learners in higher education, however, the picture is not quite so hopeful. Sissel, Hansman, and Kasworm describe the political neglect of adult learners in higher educational settings, even though on most university campuses, adult learners comprise more than 50 percent of the student body. They maintain that the politics, culture, economics, and social structures in larger society are duplicated in higher educational settings. Thus, the hegemony of the larger society plays out in higher educational settings, effectively leaving adult learners as "other," and therefore politically powerless.

So what can adult educators do politically to strengthen the positionality of adult learners in higher educational settings? As Sissel, Hansman, and Kasworm suggest, adult educators can help create privileged spaces for adult learners, acting as advocates for adult learners in whatever ways possible. Central to this advocacy is helping higher education institutions understand the needs of the adult student population within their communities while not promoting a general humanist view of adult learners that may not accurately reflect the needs of the learners within the community. Equally important is questioning policy regarding access for adult learners and promoting greater visibility of adult learning programs on campuses. All of these actions can lead to democratic practice on university campuses for adult learners.

Negotiating Power and Politics: Back to the Personal

A quick review of all the political issues and turmoil that confront adult educators in this volume might tempt one to run for the hills. As the chapter authors indicate, the political landscape of adult education is a bumpy terrain, and it is not likely to become level as long as adult educators remain separated from each other, residing in their own ideological caves. Notwithstanding the bleak landscape, however, all is not lost. There is some room for political maneuvering and strategizing, as the chapter authors have indicated. I too would like to suggest several ways of approaching the political issues confronting our field.

First, adult educators in all areas need to understand their work as inherently political. Freire (1990) reminds us that education is never neutral and is never practiced on an impartial stage (Cervero and Wilson, 2001). Defining the power issues that shape how we practice moves us toward participating fully in the political action of practice. As Sissel, Hansman, and Kasworm (Chapter Two) and others (for example, Holford, 1995; Horton and Freire, 1990; Hugo, 1990) point out, adult education as a field has a long history of political work in literacy, civil rights, the women's movement, immigration, union organizations, the environment, and many others. I suggest that we look to these historic political movements to facilitate understanding of our own roles as actors on the adult education political stage, no matter the area of adult education in which we practice. Examination of power, privilege, and knowledge concerning both macro- and micropolitics that affect and shape all areas of adult education should continue and be an essential source to help us understand power and politics in adult education more fully.

Second, as a field, we need to give up the notion of generic adult learners for whom practice principles can be easily described and prescribed. These generic descriptions lead to "one size fits all" prescriptive practices, descriptions of actions, and program planning recommendations. Adult educators must pay attention to the context in which they practice and challenge dominant and frequently hegemonic ideas concerning typical, or generic, adult learners, because these are the ideas that may set the stage for policy decisions. Graduate adult education faculty members should examine graduate program curriculum on a regular basis to make sure it recognizes and reflects the complex and changing world of adult learners. This is a political issue, not just a practice issue. The interests of both the learners and adult educators will be served when respect for the diversity and plurality of learners and the learning context is recognized.

Third, as our umbrella organization, the AAACE, struggles to find its mission, adult educators need to question the true purpose of this and similar organizations and take part in important decisions concerning their policies and procedures. Open forums are needed at meetings for members to mesh together in such debates. As adult educators, we need to become politically engaged in discourse concerning issues that surround our professional organizations and engage in collective action that leads toward policy development. This collective action could include educating and informing elected officials about key adult education legislation and policy decisions.

Finally, adult education as a field can influence the larger world only if it can recognize and respect differences, negotiate conflicts toward resolutions, and embrace broader understandings of the work of adult educators. This could include, as Wilson (Chapter Eight) suggests, collaborating and forging occupational alliances with other professions, such as nursing, legal, or teaching. In taking these actions, however, adult educators, personally and professionally, should challenge others with whom we practice by asking and answering the following questions about whatever form of adult education in which we engage: For whom? For what purpose? Who plans? Who benefits?

But we must do more than ask these questions. As adult educators, we should continually and expressly examine issues of power and domination to help adult learners overcome the hegemonic structures that keep their needs, presence, and voices absent from discussions (Giroux and Freire, 1987). We must engage in meaningful discourse—personally, organizationally, politically—across our ideological borders to clarify our identity and thus our actions through democratic practice within the field of adult education.

References

Aronowitz, S., and Giroux, H. *Postmodern Education: Politics, Culture, and Social Criticism*. Minneapolis: University of Minnesota Press, 1991.

Cervero, R. M., and Wilson, A. L. (eds.). *Power in Practice*. San Francisco: Jossey-Bass, 2001.

Cunningham, P. "Making a More Significant Impact on Society." In B. A. Quigley (ed.), *Fulfilling the Promise of Adult and Continuing Education*. New Directions for Continuing Education, no. 44. San Francisco: Jossey-Bass, 1989.

Deshler, D., and Grudens-Schuck, N. "The Politics of Knowledge Construction." In A. L. Wilson and E. R. Hayes (eds.), *Handbook of Adult and Continuing Education*. San Francisco: Jossey-Bass, 2000.

Freire, P. *Pedagogy of the Oppressed*. New York: Seabury Press, 1990.

Giroux, H., and Freire, P. "Series Introduction." In D. W. Livingstone (ed.), *Critical Pedagogy and Cultural Power*. New York: Bergin & Garvey, 1987.

Heaney, T. W. "Adult Education and Society." In A. L. Wilson and E. R. Hayes (eds.), *Handbook of Adult and Continuing Education*. San Francisco: Jossey-Bass, 2000.

Holford, J. "Why Social Movements Matter: Adult Education Theory, Cognitive Praxis and the Creation of Knowledge." *Adult Education Quarterly*, 1995, *45*, 95–111.

Horton, M., and Freire, P. *We Make the Road by Walking.* Philadelphia: Temple University Press, 1990.

Hugo, J. "Adult Education History and the Issue of Gender: Toward a Different History of Adult Education in America." *Adult Education Quarterly*, 1990, *46*, 142–157.

Imel, S., Brockett, R., and James, W. B. "Defining the Profession: A Critical Appraisal." In A. L. Wilson and E. R. Hayes (eds.), *Handbook of Adult and Continuing Education.* San Francisco: Jossey-Bass, 2000.

Podeschi, R. "Evolving Directions in Professionalization and Philosophy." In A. L. Wilson and E. R. Hayes (eds.), *Handbook of Adult and Continuing Education.* San Francisco: Jossey-Bass, 2000.

Wilson, A. L., and Hayes, E. R. (eds.). *Handbook of Adult and Continuing Education.* San Francisco: Jossey-Bass, 2000.

CATHERINE A. HANSMAN is assistant professor and program director of the M.Ed. program in adult learning and development and the leadership and lifelong learning track in the Ph.D. program in urban education at Cleveland State University, Ohio.

INDEX

SINGLE ISSUE SALE

For a limited time save 10% on single issues! Save an additional 10% when you purchase three or more single issues. Each Issue is normally $27.00.

Please see the next page for a complete listing of available back issues.

Mail or fax this completed for to: Jossey-Bass, A Wiley Company

989 Market Street • San Francisco CA 94103-1741

CALL OR FAX

Phone 888-378-2537 or 415-433-1740 *or Fax* 800-605-2665 or 415-433-4611 (*attn customer service*)

BE SURE TO USE PROMOTION CODE ND2 TO GUARANTEE YOUR DISCOUNT!

Please send me the following issues at $24.30 each.
(Important: please include series initials and issue number, such as ACE90.)

1. ACE _____

_____

_____

$ _____ Total for single issues ($24.30 each)

_____ Less 10% if ordering 3 or more issues

$ _____ Shipping charges: Up to $30, add $5.50 • $30.01–$50, add $6.50
$50.01–$75, add $7.50 • $75.01–$100, add $9 • $100.01–$150, add $10
Over $150, call for shipping charge.

$ _____ Total (Add appropriate sales tax for your state. Canadian residents add GST)

❏ Payment enclosed (U.S. check or money order only)

❏ VISA, MC, AmEx, Discover Card # _____ Exp. date _____

Signature _____

Day phone _____

❏ Bill me (U.S. institutional orders only. Purchase order required.)

Purchase order # _____

Federal Tax I.D. 135593032   GST 89102 8052

Name _____

Address _____

_____

Phone _____ E-mail _____

For more information about Jossey-Bass, visit our Web site at: www.josseybass.com

OFFER EXPIRES FEBUARY 28, 2002   **PRIORITY CODE = ND2**

yielded improvements in six different settings, including a hospital, a university and a literacy education program.

ACE70   A Community-Based Approach to Literacy Programs: Taking Learners' Lives into Account *Peggy A. Sissel*
Encouraging a community-based approach that takes account of the reality of learner's lives; this volume offers suggestions for incorporating knowledge about a learner's particular context, culture, and community into adult literacy programming. The purpose is to encourage reflection and discussion among practitioners, program developers, and policy makers as they work toward meeting the needs of their own communities of various kinds.

ACE69   What Really Matters in Adult Education Program Planning: Lessons in Negotiating Power and Interests *Ronald M. Cervero, Arthur L. Wilson*
This volume identifies issues faced by program planners in practice settings and the actual negotiation strategies they use. Contributors argue that planning is generally conducted within a set of personal, organizational, and social relationships among people who may have similar, different, or conflicting interests and the program planner's responsibility centers on how to negotiate these interests to construct an effective program.

ACE68   Workplace Learning *W. Franklin Spikes*
Increased technology, new management strategies, and reengineered and downsized organizations have caused workplace educators to rethink their craft and formulate answers to the new and immediate business issues faced by their organizations. This volume is designed to help readers examine current issues surrounding workplace learning programs and incorporate these ideas into their own professional practice.

ACE66   Mentoring: New Strategies and Challenges *Michael W. Galbraith, Norman H. Cohen*
This volume assists educators in clarifying and describing various elements of the mentoring process. It is also intended to enhance the reader's understanding of the utility, practice application, and research potential of mentoring in adult and continuing education.

ACE65   Learning Environments for Women's Adult Development: Bridges Toward Changes *Kathleen Taylor, Catherine Marienau*
This volume explores theory and practice in adult development, adult learning, and feminist pedagogy for learning environments designed to meet women's needs. The central aim of this book is to help make learning environments more supportive of reentry women in their ongoing development.

ACE62   Experiential Learning: A New Approach *Lewis Jackson, Rosemary S. Caffarella*
This volume presents discussions of a comprehensive model of experiential learning for instructors of adults in formal educational programs. Chapters argue that linking the conceptual foundations of adult and experimental learning to actual instructional applications is key to effective practice.

ACE59   Applying Cognitive Learning Theory to Adult Learning *Daniele D. Flannery*
While much is written about adult learning, basic tenets of cognitive theory are often taken for granted. This volume presents an understanding of basic cognitive theory and applies it to the teaching-learning exchange.

ACE57   An Update on Adult Learning Theory *Sharan B. Merriam*
This volume presents discussions of well-established theories and new perspectives on learning in adulthood. Knowles' andragogy, self-directed learning, Mezirow's perspective transformation, and several other models are assessed for their contribution to our understanding of adult learning. In addition, recent theoretical orientations, including consciousness and learning, situated cognition, critical theory, and feminist pedagogy, are discussed.